Stephen

Blessed are
and thirst for
they will be

Hope you enjoy. Every
blessing
        Peter   20.12.19

Life IN
PIECES!

*Practical Poetry, Prose, Prayer
and Prophecy*

PETER J. FARLEY

xulon
PRESS

To Margaret, my most ardent critic,
in recognition of her long-suffering endurance of me
and my multifarious foibles.

ACKNOWLEDGEMENTS

A ccording to Locard's exchange principle, wherever someone has been, they will always leave minute particles of evidence that they have been there because wherever we go, we take something away and leave something behind. This is one of the basic tenets of forensic science.

In my experience, this principle holds true for life itself. If physical particles will undoubtedly have been exchanged, even in the most fleeting of encounters, how much more have I taken away, albeit less tangible or less evident, in terms of understanding, wisdom, knowledge and experience from those I have come into contact with, known or still know. In addition, how much have I been given in love, joy, empathy, compassion, understanding, tolerance and acceptance. All these have influenced me and for these precious gifts, I am extremely grateful. I realise too, I have left so much behind. I rejoice where anything has been a blessing but I ask for forgiveness where it has caused sorrow, regret, sadness or even bitterness.

If I had to acknowledge all the people who have contributed to my life, I could fill many pages. So, can I just say thank you to my family, my friends and indeed anyone who has brought into my life, gifts of wholeness or healing of body, soul or spirit.

Lastly (but also firstly), I acknowledge the debt I owe, far above all others, to my Creator. For all He has given me, the greatest thanks to God — my Heavenly Father; Jesus, my ever faithful Friend, Lord and Saviour; and The Holy Spirit, as the instigator of anything of any worth in my life and certainly the One who inspired me to write. To Him be the Glory!

TABLE OF CONTENTS

PREFACE

Dear Reader

I just wanted to take the opportunity to say 'Hi' and explain a little about *Life in Pieces!* The original title was: *Practical Poetry, Prose, Prayer and Prophecy.* I think you will agree, this does not exactly roll off the tongue or grab a potential reader's attention on the bookshelf. *Life in Pieces!* on the other hand is pithy, and in all probability would be more likely to attract a second look from those who I hope would enjoy reading it — perhaps it did you!. However, both titles are apt. *Life in Pieces!* is a collection of pieces of poetry, prose, prayer and prophecy — written during my life!

Why then did I choose the lengthier title: *Practical Poetry, Prose, Prayer and Prophecy?* Basically, I wanted to dispel the myth, that to write anything of any value, the author needs to be intellectual or academic. Rather, a writer could be anyone who has learned, even to the most rudimentary level, to read and write. Think about a young child, proudly taking home from school, something they have drawn, painted or even written, to show Mummy or Daddy. What does the parent instinctively do? They express delight at what has been produced, putting it up in a prominent place, for others to admire. Certainly, they do not pass judgement on style, craftsmanship or artistic skill; nor do they criticise content, accuracy or neatness. Instead, by their words and actions, they let the child see the value they place on their early attempts at creative endeavour. For me, that is how God views and accepts our attempts at self-expression.

'In my book', writing is an act of self-expression, something you are creating, for yourself and for God. To emphasise this, at the end of the book (where it is supposed to go!) you will find a postscript. I hope you will find this an incentive to have a go, an encouragement to believe you can find (and give) pleasure, in putting pen to paper or tapping away at a keyboard.

Righting writing!

It took me two attempts (or was it three?) to pass my 'O' Level exam in English Language (equivalent of a High School Diploma in the States) and I am sure this was an indication that writing was not my natural forte. Over the intervening years though, for whatever reason, having been forced to put things in writing, I believe my composed efforts have improved. Increasingly, aided by my innate love of words, I have found great enjoyment in committing my thoughts and impressions to paper, be it in poetry or prose.

For me, the process of writing, is in itself both cathartic and sufficiently satisfying. It is a bonus if others find my efforts of interest or enjoyment. Even so, it is not without trepidation that I have decided to publish some of my work. I trust there will be those who will find pleasure in reading it. If all it does, is to induce others to think:

'I could do as well or better than that' and inspire them to do so, that will be reward enough.

Poetry or Prose?

How does poetry differ from prose? In many cases, it's easy to differentiate between the two, especially when poetry is laid out in verses and more so when certain lines in the poem intentionally rhyme with each other. In many cases though, the distinction is unclear and the boundaries between the two forms of written expression are blurred. At least, that's how it seems to me. I am sure literary experts could more easily separate the two.

What bearing does this dichotomy have on this book? In the main, I have set the remainder of the book in four sections — one each for poetry, prose, prophecy and prayer. I have then placed pieces of writing, in the section I think they belong. However I am far from sure that I have classified them correctly. Well, such was my own uncertainty, I decided to select what I thought was a definite example of each and place it before the main sections. I leave it to others to decide what they think.

What is prophecy?

There many answers to this question, and much will depend on who is setting forth the answer. For many, prophecy is usually seen, as simply a prediction of the future. Others will say, a study of the messages of prophets in the Bible, especially the minor prophets, will show prophecy is more about the present, than predicting the future. There is general agreement that a 'prophet' communicates messages he claims he has received, through divine revelation.

Within churches where prophecy is an accepted medium for God to communicate with His people, prophecy is seen as words spoken (or in some cases sung), which the 'prophet' believes are spontaneous, personal revelations from The Holy Spirit. These are given to encourage, exhort, edify, inspire, guide, and sometimes, convict fellow believers. More rarely, such words may speak of future events. This is generally how I would answer the question.

However, I believe being prophetic has a much wider meaning. Put simply, I see prophecy as a demonstration or declaration of God's desired state for His creation, and His people. This would mean our lives are meant to be prophetic; our actions, our attitudes, our values and our lifestyle, as well as our words (spoken in everyday life), should declare the Kingdom of God.

In this book, I have included what I believed were spontaneous revelations to me, from The Holy Spirit, to encourage, exhort, edify, inspire, guide and even convict, my brothers and sisters in Christ. For prophetic words to be received as such, they need to be weighed by those hearing them. Individuals must then decide, whether God has spoken through those words, to them.

May I though, encourage you the reader, as I encourage myself, to make every effort to ensure that, as much as possible, our every action, our every deed, as well as our every word, is a manifestation of God's kingdom, and a demonstration of His love, His mercy, His grace, His Goodness and His holiness. If we do this, we will, I believe, be truly prophetic — indeed, predicting the age to come.

Why has he written that?

I have written notes about some of the items and indeed the sections, in order to aid appreciation of my intent. I have found that God does work all things together for good, in that He has used seemingly negative experiences in my life for positive effect Mary Cholmondeley is quoted as saying: *Sorrow with his pick mines the heart. But he is a cunning workman. He deepens the channels whereby happiness may enter, and hollows out new chambers for joy to abide in, when he is gone.* So it has been that sorrow has sometimes been the catalyst for me to more earnestly commit my thoughts to paper. The sweet poignancy of such events continues to have a great impact on my life. One of the ways it has done so, is to enhance the melancholic in me, which I believe characterises and provokes much creative endeavour.

I hope I have succeeded in my writing, to weave together many strands, such as: hope, redemption, mercy, grace, adoration and wonder. This I believe is an indication of how God has woven so many of His blessings and His provision into my life. The miraculous truth is that, given the opportunity, God will also weave Himself into our lives — truly Immanuel, God with us, in us and through us. I hope that is also seen in what I have written herein.

I read a poem many years ago and I don't know who the author was, but part of it went something like this:

God is not man, that in the day of His coming, He would say,
"You should have better understood and known the evil from the good."
But if with purpose true today, I seek but seem to lose the way,
Yet am I, in the courts above, judged by the perfect law of love.

Maybe people could pick theological holes in such a statement but for me it indicates something of the heart of God, as I understand and know it — which I find a great comfort and consolation. Ultimately, God judges my heart and motives and though I can get things wrong, graciously, as

Adrian Rogers of the Billy Graham Evangelistic Association states (echoing Romans 8: 28) 'God can take things that are bad and put them in the crucible of His wisdom and love. He works all things together for good, and He gives us the glorious, wonderful promise that He will do so'.

Developing the inner child

Mostly, the poetry section is in chronological order. It is interesting for me to note that my early poetical work seems trapped in rhyme and characterised by my frustration in my perceived inability to adequately express my feelings. Then the point comes, where my writing is released into a freer form and the spiritual dimension becomes more marked. Many readers will I am sure notice, that some of my work is written as though by a child. For me this is a significant characteristic, for it is an indication of the importance I attach to acknowledging the child within, the little boy at the core of my being. I am so grateful that above all else, I see myself as a child of God, probably somewhere between the ages of four and eight!

Two sides of the coin!

As I was writing this, a picture came into my mind of a British Pound coin. On the one side, 'heads', is the head of the Queen — Elizabeth the Second. This is always the same. If you are British, you instantly know it is a 'coin of the realm'. The reverse side, 'tails', will vary. It could be a coat of arms, a national emblem or a monument. The tails sides of British Two-Pound coins are even more varied. In 2016, the Royal Mint produced three Two-Pound coins to commemorate the 400th anniversary of Shakespeare's death. Anniversaries of The Great Fire of London in 1666 and the Battle of Hastings in 1066 also feature on the tails side of Two Pound coins produced this year.

Why do I mention this? It reminds me that in many ways, I am like a British pound coin. There are two sides to me as a Christian. The one side, which depicts God, is constant. The reverse side, which depicts me, varies. In fact, it can change from moment to moment, dependent on my mood, my attitude, my choosing. Life is not a question of chance, a case of tossing a coin. It is a matter of choice. I can choose which side is seen most in my life but that does not mean I am more ashamed of the other side. The Sovereign's Head shows whose coinage it is. The true value of the coin is shown on the 'tails' side — one Pound. My 'heads' side shows who I belong to. My 'tails' side shows the value God puts on me.

It is a wonderful privilege to be chosen, to be put on the reverse side of God's coin. However, it is a privilege enjoyed by all those who put their trust in Jesus. This particular coin has been around a long time. It is showing signs of wear, maybe a few scratches and even chips. Maybe you think it is slightly grubby. What matters though, is it belongs to God and always will do. All the same, I hope you enjoy what you see of me, as you read this book. God bless you.

Peter Farley
February 2016

PROLOGUE

My story, His story

Creation

I believe we were all created to create; there is something uniquely satisfying in completing a task, especially if that task is conceived in the imagination. Whenever someone finishes some creative endeavour, its completion brings great satisfaction and contentment. To give substance to the aesthetic seems to meet an elemental need. I make no claim to have any great artistic skill or creative ability but even so, I feel the need to actualise the abstractions I sense within.

In Genesis 1, after finishing His creation, *'God saw all that he had made, and it was very good'* – Genesis 1:31. For me, this is the first record of the importance of ensuring quality in creating, as in all our endeavours. I believe God set for us the benchmark for quality — to be able to look at what we've created and say it is very good. For us, as human beings, nothing we create will be perfect; it will always be flawed. I remember reading some years ago that the more we magnify the works of man, the more we see the imperfections but the more we magnify the work of God, the more we see how perfect it is. Magnify anything in creation and see if this is not so.

In the beginning: God.

To set my work in context, you as the reader, will need to appreciate that I have always been conscious God was in my life. From my birth, my name was on the cradle-roll of my local Baptist Church. From the age of three, I went to Sunday School on Sunday afternoons. There I learned songs and choruses and listened to many Bible stories. When I was old enough to go, I went to the morning service at church and again, when I was old enough, I started going to the evening service, too. I went, not because I was taken or made to go but because I wanted to go.

None of this meant I was a Christian but the message I heard, was consistently the message of grace. I came to understand very early, that God was my loving Heavenly Father and that He had sent His Son to be the Saviour of the world. I learned many Bible verses by heart but none summarises the message of grace more succinctly than John 3:16.

For God so loved the world that he gave his one and only Son, that whoever believes in him shall not perish but have eternal life.

I don't know the exact date I asked Jesus into my heart as my personal Saviour. I think probably, every time there was an invitation to do so (between when I was three and when I was eight), my hand went up. I'm sure God smiled every time and I'm also certain that one of those times, if not every time, my name was written in the *Lamb's Book of Life*!

I do know that at the age of ten, I was interviewed on a national radio show. I still have the newspaper cutting about the show, which recounts how I told the person interviewing me (a renowned broadcaster), that when I grew up, I wanted to be a missionary. At the time, much inspired by Jim Elliott and Nate Saint, I was passionate about Amazonia and I thought this could mean God wanted me to be a missionary in South America. The way in which that call on my life came to fruition though, forty years later, is further evidence of God's mercy and grace.

The Gift of God

In Spring 1981, I woke up at twenty to six one morning, and the idea for a project to help young people, literally cascaded into my mind. I was certain this was God-given. This idea became known as The Matthew Project–'Matthew' meaning 'the Gift of God'. Some two years later, after the seed had gone into the ground, and died, God revived this vision, and I was encouraged to wait on him, as to the next step.

One thing I have never been very good at is waiting on God in prayer, but I can remember, one particular sunny morning, taking my deckchair out into the garden, determined to sit there for as long as it took, to hear from Him. God was very gracious. Knowing of my inability to persevere in prayer, within a few minutes of sitting down, having said to Him that I was into praying for the long-haul, I felt Him say that The Matthew Project was a fulfilment of His call on my life, as a child, to be a missionary. So it wasn't to the Auca Indians but to the young (and not so young) people of Norwich (where I was living at the time), who were suffering as a result of drug or alcohol abuse, and to whom God was calling me to go.

Today, over thirty years on, The Matthew Project has around 130 staff and, over the years, has provided substance abuse help, support and treatment for thousands of young people, their families and friends. We have also seen God supply millions of pounds to fund this work. For further information about their activities, visit www.matthewproject.org

In the end: God.

There are many things I don't understand but at the risk of sounding arrogant, there isn't a question I don't know the answer to. Truly, whenever there is a question myself or others find difficult to answer, I have learned the only answer that makes sense is: 'God'. I am confident he is the answer because my Heavenly Father is an all loving, all powerful, all knowing God.

In the ESV, Isaiah 26:3 states: '*You keep him in perfect peace whose mind is stayed on you because he trusts in you.*' Another version of that verse reads: '*You will keep him in soundness of health whose imagination stops at God.*' Here health is the Hebrew word Shalom, which comes from the root verb shalom meaning to be complete, perfect and full. *Shalom*, according to Strong's Concordance, has a very wide and varied meaning. It is completeness, wholeness, health, peace, welfare, safety, soundness, tranquillity, prosperity, perfectness, fullness, rest, harmony, the absence of agitation or discord.'

I have found, as have many others, whenever I am troubled, confused, perplexed, uncertain of the future, unsure of which way to turn, it is pointless to let my mind run away into endless uncertainty and speculation. Rather, I have determined to let my imagination stop at God. So, rather than imagine I shall be alright if this happens, or that happens, instead of looking for other ways out of my trouble, I say to myself: Everything will work out right because GodFULLSTOP or, as the Americans would say: Everything will work out right because GodPERIOD.

Childlike, naïve trust it may be, but for me, it has stood the test of time, surviving every intellectual challenge. No matter how intelligent a person is, no matter how much knowledge they have, no matter how learned they are – it all comes down to faith. I have not been indoctrinated, I have not been duped but I have received, experienced and appreciated such overwhelming subjective evidence, that the erudite offerings of the most renowned atheists are found wanting in comparison.

Anyway, that's me — here's the rest of the book!

P.S. **Author's Warning:** To get the most out of this book, would readers indulge me by setting aside for a while, normally very valid conventions such as the Chicago Manual of Style. Doing so will hopefully allow the idiosyncrasies of my writing to be seen, without detracting from the enjoyment of reading my work. I trust this will encourage would-be writers to initially just express what is in their mind or on their heart and let grammatical correctness come later. For this reason I have not, on this occasion, made use of the excellent copy editing services offered by Xulon Press. Also, please excuse the anglicised rather than the anglicized spellings!

Why is it? – A poem

Why is it Lord, when I feel so far away from You,
You can make me feel You're so near?
Why is it Lord, when I feel there's no future,
You can make me feel life has just begun?
Why is it Lord, when I feel there's a happy ending,
You can make me feel it's just a new beginning?

Why is it Lord, when I feel the storm clouds gathering,
You can make me feel the sky's so blue?
Why is it Lord, when I feel so unworthy,
You can make me feel so accepted?
Why is it Lord, when I feel so soiled,
You can make me feel so cleansed?

Why is it Lord, when I feel so small,
You can make me feel You're so big?
Why is it Lord, when I feel my heart is breaking,
You can make me feel my soul is bursting?
Why is it Lord, when I feel like crying,
You can make me feel like laughing?

Why is it Lord?

**Why is it child, when I want you to feel my presence,
You want to put yourself beyond the pale?
Why is it child, when I want to give you an answer,
You want to ask me a question?
Why is it child, when I want you to bask in the sunlight of my love.
You want to hide in the shadow of rejection?**

**Why is it child, when I want to wash you in mountain streams,
You want to wallow in the silt of stagnant waters?
Why is it child, when I want to deck you in garlands of flowers,
You want to festoon yourself in a tangle of weeds?
Why is it child, when I want so much for you,
You want to settle for so little?**

Why is it child?

I don't know why it is, Lord.
I know why it is, child.

I don't understand, Lord.
I understand, child.

Do you mean You love me, Lord?
I mean I love you, child.

Thank You, Lord.
Thank you, child.

Lord?
Child?

Lord.
Child.

Why, Lord?
Why not, Child?

Sin, Shame, Sense, Salvation

Hanging there, it looked so tempting, as it always did. In my mind's eye, I could picture me enjoying its seductive succulence. I imagined tasting its sweetness, as the abundant, syrupy juice dribbled down my chin. I had no choice, or so I told myself in that mad moment.

With eager hand, I reached up to pluck it. I looked at it once more, and thought it looked delicious. My fingers closed around it, before with stubborn, sinful determination, I took a bite. And oh, it was so sweet. Avidly, I gorged myself, unable it seemed to get enough.

As it slipped down into my inner being, that oh so familiar taste of nausea and sense of shame welled up in me. The heartburn of guilt discomforted me, as though there was a reflux of my spirit, revealing my stupidity and sin.

Suddenly, I heard the voice of the Father, calling out, "Peter, where are you?" Where could I hide? Somewhere I could see, without being seen, how angry God was with me. Dropping the fruit, I climbed up into the nearest sycamore tree, as far as I could get — up into the foliage. There, I would be hidden from view.

Below me, I could hear the sound of someone moving. Looking down, I saw a figure reaching down to pick up the discarded evidence of my iniquity. I drew back further into my hiding place. It was then I heard the voice of the Spirit, behind me, in the tree. "Peter, we knew where you were, but we needed you to realise you cannot flee from us. Look down."

I looked down, and saw the face of Jesus, looking up at me — a smile, almost of amusement, on his face. He called out, "Peter, come down immediately! I want you to come with me, for I have prepared a feast for you."

I realised how stupid, stubborn and sinful I had been. Eagerly, almost unbelieving, I climbed down, and fell at his feet, weeping with sorrow.

Pleadingly, I cried out, "Lord, I have sinned and am no longer worthy to be called your son."

The Lord reached down and pulled me to my feet. Head bowed, the tears still rolling down my cheeks, I found myself saying, "Lord, I am sorry. Once again, I have let you down. More than that, I have grieved your heart. Please forgive me."

It was then He said, "Peter, as many times as you confess your sin, I am faithful and just and will forgive you everything, cleansing you from all unrighteousness. Now come, and walk with me in the light, so that we can have fellowship together. Always remember, my blood purifies you from all sin. Remember too, you have no need to try and hide from God, for nothing in all creation is hidden from Me. In any case, your life is now hidden with Me in God."

At this, my heart leapt with joy, as once again I realised, that therefore there is now no condemnation for me because I am in Christ Jesus. I rejoiced too, knowing that my transgressions were forgiven and my sins covered — how blessed I then was. I called to mind though, how so often in my sin, I kept silent. At such times, it was as though my bones were wasting away, through my groaning all day long. It seemed as though, throughout the day and even at night, God's heavy hand of conviction was on me. It felt as it does in the height of summer, that the heat was sapping away my strength.

It was then, like now, as I acknowledged my sin to God, and did not look to hide myself and my iniquity, I found relief. I recalled too, how, immediately I confessed my transgressions to the Lord, he forgave the guilt of my sin. Surely, the secret, when I felt I was drowning in my sinfulness, was to turn in faith to God, and confess that I had grieved Him. It was then I would know, the mighty, rising waters of condemnation could never completely overwhelm me. Truly, God was my hiding place, and He would protect me from trouble.

Suddenly, I heard Jesus say, "I will instruct you and teach you in the way you should go; I will counsel you and watch over you. You need not suffer the woes of the wicked, for My unfailing love will surround you, if you will just trust in me." Wonderfully, He burst into song, singing anthems of deliverance.

I could not hold back, and so it was, I found myself singing a song of rejoicing, which only the righteous can sing. As we walked together, side by side, our voices harmonised. I knew I was walking with the One called Joy, being led by the One called Peace. Little surprise then, the mountains and hills we walked through, burst into song and the trees of the field began to clap their hands. It was, as if the whole creation was on tiptoe, waiting to see the wonderful sight of this particular son of God, coming into all the Father had for him.

Turning to the One who walked beside me, I found myself saying, "Lord, you alone are my portion and my cup; you make my lot secure. The boundary lines have fallen for me in pleasant places; surely I have a delightful inheritance. May I keep my eyes always on You. With You at my right hand, I will not be shaken. Therefore, my heart is glad and my tongue rejoices; my body also rests secure. You have made known to me the path of life; you fill me with joy in your presence. I now know goodness and mercy will follow me all the days of my life and I will dwell in Your house forever."

At this the Lord looked at me and a glorious smile spread across His face, a smile of love, a smile of mercy — a knowing smile. I heard Him say, "You are right Peter, for I am preparing a place for you in My Father's house and one day I will come and take you to be with me, that you also may be where I am.

An Unbeliever's Prayer

I pray to you, so I must think you are there. Therefore, I will imagine you are there. If I imagine you are there, who do I think you are? What do I think you might be able to do for me?

To be what I need you to be, you would need to know everything about me. I think it is said you are omniscient — all-knowing. I must believe that to be the case, otherwise why would I bother praying to you, and I know I am praying.

I heard someone say, one of the names you call yourself is 'I AM'. I think they also said you were omnipresent — everywhere, that you were the same yesterday, today and forever. If that is true, you are there, you are here — always have been, always will be.

Are you there to listen to my cry? I believe you are. Why would you be listening to my cry though? Is it to ignore me, to not answer me? I can't believe it is, therefore I will believe you'll answer me

When will you answer my prayer? How will you answer my prayer? When do I imagine you will answer my prayer? How do I imagine you will answer my prayer?

If you are all-knowing (and I think I believe you are), you will know the right time and the right way to answer my prayer. I guess I just have to trust you, which is what I think I'm doing now.

How can I know you have heard my prayer? Perhaps you are giving me that assurance, by answering me through my questions now, as quietly and confidently, I am trusting you to do just that.

Thank you God — I think!

Bring me – A prophecy

The very things you think disqualify you, are the very things that qualify you. The very things you consider I'll reject, are the very things I'll accept from you. The very things you believe I won't want, are the very things I ask you to bring. So come and lay them before me and let me, by laying my hand on them, change them – for I am the God who transforms.

Bring me your poverty
and I will transform it into your wealth.
Bring me your weakness
and I will transform it into your strength.
Bring me your ignorance
and I will transform it into your wisdom.
Bring me your inadequacy
and I will transform it into your sufficiency.

Bring me your timidity
and I will transform it into your tenacity.
Bring me your fear
and I will transform it into your peace.
Bring me your turmoil
and I will transform it into your contentment.
Bring me your sickness
and I will transform it into your health.

Bring me your fickleness
and I will transform it into your resilience.
Bring me your sorrow
and I will transform it into your joy.
Bring me your uncertainty
and I will transform it into your sureness.
Bring me your sinfulness
and I will transform it into your holiness.

POETRY
(I think!)

In the prologue, I indicated that God can use seemingly negative events, for positive effect. So perhaps a few words of explanation might be helpful, concerning some of my writing. When my first marriage ended in divorce, my oldest daughter, Caroline, was nearly eight. I decided that it was best if I didn't have ongoing contact with her and her younger sister. I reasoned that if I kept on seeing them, it might confuse them and cause them more heartache than having a clean break. In any case, might it not have been better for them to make a fresh start?

In hindsight, I wonder whether this was the right decision — I doubt it. One of the consequences was that I had no contact with Caroline, for over twenty years. Then one day, right out of the blue, she made contact with me, and we were gloriously reunited – but that's another story. This may suggest then, how and why I came to write particular poems.

Strand of Childhood Revisited

Life's river now has widened some, its waters running deep;
Swelled with a tide of memories, that only stills with sleep.
Yet oft I find I'm turning back, back to an earlier year,
To cascade over memories, which hold not any fear.

The river then was just a stream, that ran so fast and free,
Yet every day, with added force, moved on towards the sea.
I walk along a silent strand, and live again the day,
When, all in childhood innocence, I ventured there to play.

I see again an iron bridge, another made of stone
And in between an island — recluse, yet not alone.
There, around its shadowy banks, the water laps its song,
And, with the lowering of the tide, the rivulets tinkle on.

I hear again the many sounds that make the picture whole,
The rustling of the willow trees, the tug boat's haunting toll.
I see again, as if a child, the artist with his brush.
He's conscious of the beauty there, oblivious to life's rush.

I search again the rough-hewn steps, to see if minnows still,
Caught by fast retreating tides, the stony crannies fill.
I feel again the zephyrs blow and hear the moorhen's cry.
I sense again the majesty the swans gave, gliding by.

I smell again the resined air, of timber on the dock,
Perfume of a bygone day, my senses now unlock.
I touch again the granite posts that guard the river's shore,
Living again those moments, from my memory's store.

Now as my course meanders on, when I feel the need of peace,
Just dwelling on that well-loved strand, gives life a brighter lease.

Thoughts on being apart from the one I love, for some months

If only I could see again, the radiance of your eyes,
That brilliant sun-like passion, to brighten my dark skies.

For skies which should see little cloud, are really overcast.
While you're away, no single day can ever go too fast.

Though clouds may hide an azure sky, abridge the daystar's track,
The thought of seeing you again, will gild my sombre rack.

The firmament will be afire, when you again I see
And then you'll find a rainbow form, the rain my tears will be.

But soon the mists will roll away, to show the ether fair,
And with the passing of the clouds, will go all worthless care.

Yet on that day, that glorious day, this time will be worthwhile,
For it will just intensify the sunlight of your smile.

Slave of Melancholy

I'm fettered by a tongue, which cannot find the fashion,
In which to house those feelings, that hunger for expression.

Drenched in joy, soaked in sadness, ecstasy fused with sorrow,
Why needs pathos so supreme, its fluency to borrow.

When wistfulness so glorious, in quiescence visits me,
I accede to its dominion, as the beach does to the sea.

No maestro born has captured, the music of my heart.
How could I hope to score it, when so lacking in the art.

Though were it ever transposed, imprisoned in the stave,
To that melody I'd listen, an ever willing slave.

But for me to just appraise it, would be such utter folly;
So forever I remain–A slave of melancholy.

Dream Substantiated

(On being reunited with a daughter after over 20 years apart)

Down thro hollow halls of yesterday, I searched for you.
In empty fields of childhood, I sought after you.
Where were you child — for I would have played with you,
Turned aside and stayed with you?

Would you have danced with me, merrily skipped with me,?
Not wanting to lose me, hide and seek chased me?
With a kiss surprised me, with daisy chains bound me?
Cried out with joy, whenever you found me?

And yet, though you sought me, I remained out of sight.
When frightened you called out, I was deaf to your plight.
Not once did I reach out, to put strong arms around you,
For dreams were the only place I could have found you.

* * * * * * *

Now seeing you child, clad in maturity,
No longer lost in mists of obscurity;
In the hollow halls of yesterday, suddenly I glimpse you,
Midst empty fields of childhood, finally I find you.

So we can finish games never started,
Now we're together, henceforth never parted.

What mystery is this?

We meet as intimate strangers, who've grown together in parting. The dissipating years strengthened our love, joining our hearts, as time broke them .

What mystery is this, that pain should conceive such joy, sorrow give birth to such bliss, and fantasy bring forth such reality?

How can the tender child be torn, and yet in the woman appear so whole. How can emotions recede for twenty years, yet rise to fullness in a moment?

As I address the woman, I speak to the child. As I gaze on the splendour of maturity, I glimpse the innocence of the maiden.

TOUCHED NEGATIVES
(Thoughts on looking back through the albums of lost years)

Would that I could develop those misty images,
Phantom memories rather than fading realities.
Collected cameos conjured by contrition,
Fevered futilities of frustrated fatherhood.

Self-barred from possessing filial mementoes,
Birthright relinquished, cheated through choice.
Captured contrivances, created to compensate;
Perchance portrayals, ponderings to placate.

Montages of might-have-beens, mask empty pages,
Discounted consequences, with fantasy gilt.
Tempting and tantalising, tortuously teasing,
Wilfully made wistful, wantonly wasted.

But now in our finding, majestic in mystery,
Ghostly galleries in rehung splendour;
Portraits of promise, pregnant with possibility,
Vicarious visions, covering vain voids.

Imprisoned expression

Struggling to harness the unrestrainable,
Trying to trap with words: the inexpressible,
Frustrated by attempts to net the phantoms of feeling,
Fearful they will prove forever illusive.
Is it that I seek the undiscoverable,
Would ensnare the indefinable, capture the uncatchable?
Torn by the hounds of failure,
Held fast by despair — whilst the quarry escapes.

Do I ask too much to reproduce my heart,
To pen my being with words?
When you see me, can you sense I bleed,
Haemorrhaging from self-inflicted gashes?
As the life-blood of emotion seeps through my skin,
My loins feel awash with that precious flood.
My mind (mocking) looks on, whilst witness to my misery,
My intellect, impotent, stands by.

Be not content with what you see,
But rather urge me to reveal the concealed,
To open the shame-sealed book, to break the muting chains,
To tear down the curtains that hide me.
I am not what you see, for I publish myself poorly.
Pity me sufficiently, to spare a prospect of perfection.
Dare to believe, if only to console me,
That deep within lies a kernel of creation,

Pregnant with possibility, an embryonic expression of my essence, wombed within the shell of my inadequacy, awaiting birth, a labour of love to be realised in release.

In an instant–Humanity.

(An ode prompted by an advert for Nescafe Blend 37,
on the London Underground)

.........ining. Here we are, created from the discharge of our previous generation. Each of us the product of a sperm (chance or chosen?), impregnating desperately for survival an ovum. A minute speck, itself clinging instinctively for our life, to the uterus wall — so avoiding ignominious expulsion. In time, escaping into the captivity of a human lifespan, sentenced (perchance or predestined?) to extinction, execution adjourned *sine die*. Which brings us back to the beg......

Journey, by train, through little-known reaches of internal space in East Anglia from Liverpool Street.

As the 15:30 leaves for Norwich, he sits, slumped over his book, reading through closed eyes the passage on "Psychic Energy and Phases of Higher Consciousness".

Oblivious to my rudeness, as I try to read what is going through his mind, he continues on his ethereal journey, till summarily ejected from his astral plane, he lands back on the train, as we draw into Colchester.

Turning the pages, he reads of the coupling of our terrestrial and celestial forebears, taking off again into the clouds beyond reality, only to ditch again from his superconscious U.F.O. This time temporally tumbling to join us, as we less-adventurous mortals, draw more conventionally into Ipswich.

Before we start off, he has again departed, this time travelling in the "Creative energy model of other-life worlds". Strange though, as the train arrives at Norwich, he gets off at the same moment as his unfellowed travellers—even though he'd taken such a wide detour.

Ex — tremes

Thousands of feet above the earth — I know my feet are on the
ground of heaven.

Above the clouds — I am sitting at Your feet.

Looking down over the ocean — I find myself paddling in eternity.

Lost for words — I sing forth Your praise.

Walking in the darkest valley — I find myself on the heights.

Tossed on the waves — I am anchored in a lagoon.

Living in a hovel — I reside in a palace.

Clothed in rags — I am dressed in the finest of apparel.

Scared by nightmares — I have the sweetest of dreams.

Troubled and tormented — I discover peace and tranquillity.

Orphaned and lonely — I am fathered and befriended.

Feeling unworthy and unforgiveable — I know I am received
and accepted.

Reaching maturity — I realise I am a child.

Dying to fantasy — I am alive to reality.

Believing myself a child of sin — I accept I am an heir of righteousness.

Having finite aspirations — I am given infinite possibilities.

Content with an earthly abode — I am satisfied with an eternal home.

(Written at 35,000ft Sunday 12th. May 1996, somewhere above Africa.)

One Hit Too Many

(Written on hearing of the death of John – a heroin addict)

Only one hit, but one hit too many.
Only one hit, to take away pain.
Only one hit, it surely can't hurt.
Only one hit — now never again.

     Easter this weekend — resurrection in season.
     No time for dying — unless you are Christ.

     So why did you do it?
     What was the fuss?
     You surely weren't speeding,
     So what was the rush?

Only one hit but one hit too many.
Only one hit, to take away pain.
Only one hit, it surely can't hurt.
Only one hit — now never again.

     Spring is here, renewing life.
     A time to tend — not destroy.

     So when the shoot's upended,
     You'll find the root has died.
     The works that stopped you working,
     Promised life but lied.

Only one hit but one hit too many.
Only one hit to take away pain.
Only one hit, it surely can't hurt.
Only one hit — now never again.

Lord, did you really?

Lord, did you really create the mountains? It's kind of hard to believe you did, as I fly over them. Their scale and grandeur are difficult to comprehend, as they push up through the clouds. You must be really tall to have created anything so high. Yet they are nothing compared to the distance of the nearest star from earth.

Lord, you must be incredibly great to have placed the stars so far away. I realise now, how small and puny is the picture of you, which I had painted on the canvas of my mind. But this picture with its pitiful scale, has determined the dimensions I have given you, the dimensions of my God.

Lord I'm sorry that my impression of you has been so, so inadequate. I have lived so long with a miniscule God and have allowed that image to reduce you to a microcosm, whilst truly you are the hugest macrocosm

Lord, did you really create the oceans? It's kind of hard to believe you did, as I fly over them. Their width and depth are impossible to visualise, as they stretch out, far below me. You must be quite a size yourself, to have created anything so enormous. But these waters are nothing compared to the vast expanses of space.

Lord, you must be incredibly great to have created the oceans and stretched out the curtains of the heavens. I realise now, how small and puny is the picture of you, which I had painted on the canvas of my mind. But this picture with its pitiful scale has determined the dimensions I have given you, the dimensions of my God.

Lord, will you expand my comprehension of your immenseness, and give me a truer appreciation of how great you are. If I am to reach my potential and fulfil your purpose for my life, I need to have a far more realistic estimation of the extent to which you are able to complete the work you have begun in me.

Above Sudan

Sudan — war-torn, ravaged by internal dissonance,
I glide above you, untroubled by your conflict.
I am out of the range of your weaponry,
Unconcerned that a stray bullet might reach me,
Knowing you cannot touch me.

Sudan — starving, bleeding dying, 33,000 feet above you,
Your desperate state does not affect me.
I am beyond the pull of your desperation.
Unmoved by all that afflicts you,
Knowing you cannot touch me.

Carnival Character

Hey Lord, I've built this amazing con-trap-tion,
It's so good that, most of the time, it even fools me!
I've been working on it quite a time;
In fact as long as I can remember.

Sometimes I think I've almost finished it,
But then, when I see what others have built,
I think I'd better add some more —
Making it higher and wider.

What is it? Well it's hard to say.
I know it's not real
But it's important to pretend,
Especially for the sake of others.

It gives the impression, when I'm inside,
That I'm much bigger than I really am.
Like I say, I know it's not real
But it doesn't do any harm — does it?

After all, when I think about it,
Everyone else is doing it.
Mostly though, I forget that,
And get taken in by what I see.

It's only at times like this,
That I start to feel uncomfortable.
It's as though you see right through it,
And you know how small I really am.

Don't you think the overall effect is good though?
Didn't you say something about walking tall?
I'm sure there was something
About looking big in the eyes of men.

In any case, if no one's really taken in,
Unless they stop to think about it,
Does it really do any harm?
It's only a game after all.

What's the game called, did you say?
How about: 'Charades'?
Yes, that's it, everyone thinks life's a carnival,
And we're all taking part in a parade.

Yes, some people do take it very seriously.
Well, yes I do sometimes.
Well maybe it is, 'more often than not'
But, like I said, everyone's doing the same.

Yes I do wish I could stop pretending.
Sometimes, when I'm trying to hold everything together,
I get really frightened that the whole thing's going to collapse,
And people will see how small I really am.

I think sometimes you must know,
I'm not really that big at all.
I think you know that inside this con-trap-tion,
There's a very frightened, little boy.

I don't understand what you're saying.
Are you sure that's right?
You mean, it's only when I realise how small I am,
That I'm big enough to be like your Son?

NOT WANTED

Having reached the great age I am, I realise more and more, I have so much to be thankful about. I am blessed by a super wife, who has put up with me for over forty five years, plus five children and thirteen grand-children, brothers and sisters and their families, as well as cousins (not to mention many wonderful people I can count as friends), all of whom accept me — warts and all! Thinking about being accepted, being valued, being wanted, brought to mind a poem I wrote a number of years ago, about someone who I was able to help.

Steve, the subject of the poem, was a young man who I met many times, when he came to see me at The Matthew Project. I also met him, on some of the occasions I went into our local prison, to hold discussion groups in the Young Offenders Wing, where he sometimes resided! Steve had many problems, including drugs, but he and I became real friends, though in many ways we were so unlike. I was truly saddened, when I learned he had been found dead on the street in Norwich, early one morning. He died of a stab wound but it was never discovered, 'by whose hand he died'. However, for me, it was a tragedy, but, sadly, there were few others who shed a tear.

His story inspired this poem, as I thought about the tragic lives so many live because basically, they are not wanted – dead or alive!

Not Wanted Dead Or Alive

Conceived without love, the offspring of lust,
A foetus of rejection, carried in a reluctant womb,
Emotionally aborted — I developed.

Brought forth with bitterness, disowned and discounted,
Expelled disinherited, unwanted, unnoticed,
Bastardised and bloody — I was born.

Fed with reluctance, on milk of indifference,
Nurtured on nothingness, starved of affection,
Weaned with neglect — I grew.

Cuddled for abuse, played with and perverted,
Fondled by depravity and embraced to defile,
Terrified and toyed with — I was loved.

Drilled in dishonesty, coached to resent,
Schooled in disgrace, whilst mastering deceit,
Uncouth and illiterate — I was taught.

Confused, bruised and brutalised, ripe for corruption,
Brazen, defiant, inviting disdain,
Contemptuous, rebellious — I matured.

Suddenly — desperate in loneliness, crying out, dropping out,
Lost in the crowd, drunken and drugged,
Finally forgotten — I died.

I really meant to!

(A love-song, a lament written for my wife on the occasion of
our fortieth wedding anniversary)

There was a picture I meant to paint,
There was a song I meant to sing,
There was a stone I meant to turn,
There was a silence I meant to break,
There was a word I meant to speak
And there was a promise I meant to keep.

But I failed to paint, to sing, to turn, to break, to speak, to keep,
And so I left no memory, for you to remember that moment by.

My only hope is that God saw my unpainted picture,
That He listened to my unsung song,
That He admired my unturned stone,
That He appreciated my unbroken silence,
That He heard my unspoken word
And that He received my unkept promise.

But I did so want you to see, to listen, to admire, to appreciate,
To hear, to receive, what was conceived in heart;
Yet never birthed into your awareness.
Truly, I did mean to leave something behind,
For you to remember that moment by.

I just didn't know how I could paint,
I didn't know how I should sing,
I didn't know which stone to turn,
I didn't know when to break the silence,
I didn't know which word to speak
And I didn't know which promise I could keep,

Forgive me then, there was no memory, nothing I left behind,
For you to remember that moment by.

But one day, I will paint such pictures,
I will sing such songs,
I will turn such stones,
I will break such silences,
I will speak such words,
I will keep such promises,
That the galleries of infinity could not house them,
And eternity not be time enough to enjoy them.

For I will have learnt the art, have been taught the skill,
Have discovered the means, been given the inspiration and found the wherewithal
To weave my feelings for you, into something substantial.
Then my works, my words, my songs, my silences,
Will harmonise with those of the Bard of the Ages.

For He is the One who paints the skies,
He is the One who sang the stars into space,
He is the One who fashioned every stone,
He is the One who breaks the silence of sorrow,
He is the One who spoke creation into existence,
And He is the One who keeps every promise.

He is the high and lofty One, who inhabits eternity,
Yet put eternity into my heart,
And He it is who will make
Everything beautiful in its time.

But in the meantime, my Love, believe me,
I truly meant to leave you a memory,
For you to remember that moment by!

Do You remember Lord?

Do You remember Lord, the young lad with the five small barley loaves and the two small fishes? Of course You do! Do you remember Lord, the little boy of five or six or maybe six or seven, who wanted to hold Your hand? Of course you do!

I can still see the smile on Your face, as You reached down and took hold of his small hand. I can still see the smile in his heart, as he held Your hand. I can still see the smile in his spirit, as he began to grasp something of how big You are, how great You are.

As he held more tightly, he felt more of Your majesty, more of Your power and, most of all, more of Your Love for him. And so he squeezed more tightly the hand that flung the stars into space, the hand that created all things — and You felt it. You felt Your hand being crushed by a little boy's love. You felt his deep desire to hold Your hand and it broke Your heart.

For he didn't realise then, that the hand that held his, held a myriad such other tiny hands. Truly it was the power You had put within that multitude of small hands, when You put eternity in their hearts, that broke Your heart. It was because of this, You determined to go ahead with Your plan, to ensure that no matter how dirty a little boys hands were, they could still ask to hold Your hand.

So, You stretched out your great hands and allowed that myriad of tiny hands to nail You to a cross. Little wonder that little boy remembers how You smiled, when he asked to hold Your hand. Little wonder he remembers the smile in his heart, as he took hold of Your hand and began to grasp something of how big You are and how great You are. I'm so glad You remember!

(Written by a little boy, aged 69 years!)

Written the morning of the day I died?

When I woke this morning, did I know today was special;

Did I realise this was the day I died?

When I reached the end of my days, were there words I should have said — words of comfort, of encouragement or praise; words of love, of grace or forgiveness?

When I reached the end of my days, were there deeds I should have done — deeds of kindness, of compassion or understanding; deeds of generosity, of unselfishness or service?

When I reached the end of my days, were there thoughts I should have considered — thoughts of goodness, of purity or humility; thoughts of gentleness, of patience or integrity?

They say you can take nothing from this world but they are wrong — you can take regrets! As I walked out of this world into eternity, was I carrying a burden of what-might-have-beens? Was I weighed down with the remorse of unspoken words, undone deeds and stillborn thoughts?

But I didn't know today was special; I didn't realise today was the day I died.

But then I didn't need to know, I didn't need to realise. All I needed to do, was to pause at the start of the day and ask myself, what words could I say today — words of comfort, of encouragement or praise; words of love, of grace or forgiveness?

What deeds could I do today — deeds of kindness, of compassion or understanding; deeds of generosity, of unselfishness or service?

What thoughts should fill my mind today — thoughts of goodness, of purity or humility; thoughts of gentleness, of patience or integrity?

What a difference I could have made, to my last day in this world. I could have walked without regret into the life to come. Unburdened, I could have run down the hill into eternity, rejoicing that in the darkness of the day of my death, I had uttered words of comfort, of encouragement or praise; of love, of grace or forgiveness. I could have given birth to deeds of kindness, of compassion or understanding; of generosity, of unselfishness or service. I could have given life to thoughts of goodness, of purity or humility; of gentleness, of patience or integrity. All these, might have brightened the day of those I met, on the last day of my life.

These words, these deeds, these thoughts, were my last gifts — to all those I loved, to all those I knew. Did my gifts bring them joy, consolation, contentment, pleasure or peace? If so I have no regrets, for living the way I did — on the day I died!

Thoughts in retrospect and prospect!

I realised I had been standing at the gate for some time. I had stood there, looking out on a glorious, sunlit garden of all seasons, which stretched into the distance, as far as the eye could see. Over and beyond the garden, a vast canopy of stars covered the heavens.

Part of me longed to step through and explore this wonderful expectation. Yet, I knew the time had not come, and the rest of me just wanted to stay and continue to enjoy all I was blessed with.

There were those I loved, my family and of course so many friends and acquaintances. Indeed, there seemed too, so much I yet wanted to do; especially in expressing what was on my heart, in my soul and spirit.

Suddenly, the gate opened, and I eagerly started to step through, for I knew it was time. It was then I sensed your hand, in love, trying to restrain me, to hold me back.

Gently you felt another hand prising yours open, so I was free to move on in. Deep within yourself, you sensed that was right, though you would have wished to have held onto me longer. Forgive me then, that in my eagerness, I rushed forward, without a backward glance.

Gathering speed, I ran on into eternity — no longer tied to time. Without stopping, I paused to admire the delicate, intricate care, with which the Creator had fashioned each bloom, running still faster.

Soon like a swan, scooting over the water, I was in the air. Now flying as I had so long imagined I would, when I left my mortal ground, I reached for the threshold of the heavens. There once more, I paused to drink in the awesome sight, to appreciate the song of the stars — the handiwork of the One who had flung them all into space and who called billions of billions of them by name.

So here I am, part of me still in the garden, to which you may be closer than you think. The rest of me is far away, in the outer reaches of infinity — still with so much to see, to rejoice in and to wonder at.

Wherever I am, I can feel His closeness, the intimate presence of my Heavenly Father. Wherever you are, my desire for you, is that you would know, how close you still are to me. For now just wait, till the time comes, when the gate opens for you.

Do not fear that when it closes, it will forever cut you off from all you those you hold dear. I know it will not, for it has not cut you off from me. So, wait quietly and confidently, whilst in the meantime, you enjoy all you are blessed with — your family, friends and acquaintances. Take every opportunity to love, encourage, comfort and bless them, whilst never hesitating to express what's in your heart, your soul and spirit.

As for me, take no further thought, except to imagine in your heart, how grateful I am to have known and loved you. If then your heart grows sad that we are apart, allow yourself to believe I am having the time of my life, for I am — forever!

PROSE

(At least, again I think so!)

Enforced Confinement

The day was bright and clear but I saw it through a mist, Tears of four thousand days upon four thousand days, and more. The pain of a freshly opened wound, numbed me to melancholy content.

Child there is much I could say and some things I might do, to cool your fevered heart. Yet, whilst you are tossed by confusion, I am fettered, chained by distance and cruelly clamped by fear. I am afraid to reach out and release the healing power of love, lest its potency should cause you to start, and, like a frightened fawn, to flee.

How long can these emotions, which I for years so cruelly dammed, be held back, unnaturally contained. It may have seemed that clumsy attempts, erected in the haste of a bygone day, would always stem their flow. But deeper, then unknown, desires, ensured that amnion of yester-year would not withstand this present surge. Do not fear the fierce tide of feeling; allow yourself to be carried on its flood, for it will not harm you.

Now I see what was conceived in that supposed severing of the cord. Through the slaughter, life lived on, as embryo-like you lodged in my soul. But now, I feel the discomfort of your long enforced confinement and understand more fully, the mystery of the life of love. When the waters burst, through the trauma, you will be brought forth, out of the womb of a father's passion—emotionally reborn.

Thinking he was the gardener....

I am a garden. Indeed, a garden within a garden and a garden within that. I have spent every day of my life, wandering in that garden. Some days I have walked about with willing purpose. On other days, I have grudgingly walked out of duty, refusing to look at the beauty around me. Thankfully, on fewer days, I have walked with eyes cast down in shame, afraid lest I should see the damage my wanton rampages have caused. Yet most days, I walk rejoicing in what I find is growing there.

I am not a gardener. Sometimes, it seems there is little I can do, to cultivate and tend my garden. I understand, a little, how others say things grow in gardens but how things really grow in my garden, remains a mystery, a mystery my limited intellect cannot grasp. Yet I know I have a duty of care, to put my finite understanding to work, to do what I can to make my garden a finer place, a tranquil place of beauty for all to enjoy.

Friend, I invite you into my outer garden. The gates are always open but you must take me as I am. Hopefully, you will find paths that will lead to acceptance, paths that will lead to friendship, to love, to peace, to joy and even perchance to healing.

I have nothing to hide but if you would look for them, hidden behind shrubbed screens, you will find the concealed, decaying remains of my frailty, the composting piles of my weaknesses, my errant ways, my failures and my foibles. Then you will discover: '*Lilies that fester, smell far worse than weeds.*' Please, I beg you, in pity look away and think not the less of me.

If you walk further into my garden, you will reach the gates of the first inner garden. I cannot stop you looking into that garden now. The only way I could have stopped you, was at the outer gate
but it's too late for that. I have invited you this far.

As I get to know and trust you, I will unlock the gates of that inner garden and allow you to wander further. Here too, you might chance upon shrubbed screens, Look behind them, if you feel you must. I would not pretend that all is as you see at first. There are places though, where few can go, parts of the garden where only those born and bonded by blood-right or joined by intimacy and invitation can frequent.

Even here, in this open, yet restricted, place, there is a secluded, pre-cluded area, where I can walk with the one who alone has the love-right. Long have we walked here, sometimes alone but most times together. Here I can almost be completely myself, almost completely open but fear prevents me revealing all. Forgive me, my love but I cannot let you fully see me as I am.

It is then, when I need to most, I reach the gate of the innermost garden. Again, others may look through the gate and perchance will see the One who resides there. For He has promised those who seek Him will find Him. Friend, child, lover, this gate is locked to all but me. For it is never locked to me. Each time I near it, the gate senses my approach and opens for me.

Immediately I enter, I notice the air is sweeter, the perfume stronger, the atmosphere drenched in peace, the garden bathed in the warmth of acceptance, of understanding, of forbearance, of forgiveness, of mercy and of grace. I know here I can be myself — completely. Here I can cast off the shame, the fear, the self-soiled, world-begrimed apparel and finally be who I am, what I am. In the nakedness of innocence, I am back in the garden where I was first created and I know someone sees what He has made and I hear His voice say, "It is very good".

Now I know I am fully known. I am *'the garden of His delight'* for in the centre of the innermost garden, is the place where the gardeners reside. There is the One who designed and created the garden. He never leaves that place and yet, when I care to be aware of it, His presence fills the garden. Indeed, in Him, I live and move and have my being.

Then there is the One who openly works in the garden. Sometimes, rich times, I work with Him, sensing His love of the garden and His joy at the beauty He cultivates, the blossoms and the fruit He works to produce, in my garden. So why are there times when I prevent Him from working and why does He allow me to do so? Surely, it is His garden and He can do as He wishes, when He wishes. And yet, He does allow me to stop Him in His labour of love. Why?

The answer is the third One. He it is who works unseen, unnoticed. His labour in the garden is ceaseless, it cannot be disturbed or disrupted. I stop on the busiest of days or the quietest, sense His presence and know He is at work. Sometimes, I even hear Him, faintly, silently, unseen, working in my soul. At these times, I know the whole garden is permeated by a scent of peace, by a sense of His presence.

He saw me erect each shrubbed screen, in a futile attempt to hide the decaying remains of my frailty, the composting piles of my weaknesses, my errant ways, my failures and my foibles. His nostrils sensed that my lilies had festered far worse than weeds. But, He didn't look away or think the less of me. Instead, I heard him say, "Son, let's take this rotten compost and use it to fertilise something which will blossom for eternity, its sight and scent giving me great and eternal pleasure. Trust me, for I can and will, work all things for the good of those who love me."

Then I said, "Lord, that would be very good!"

And He replied, "Son, I hoped that is what you would say."

I turned to Him and noticed that He was walking in the light, He was the light and I was walking with Him. Thus it was, we walked together, in the cool of the day; a child and his Heavenly Father, in fellowship with one another. I found myself going out with joy and being led forth in peace. The mountains and hills burst out into song before us, singing, "The Lord has made everything beautiful in its time and it is very good." As they did, the morning stars sang together with them, all the angels shouted for joy and all the trees of the field clapped their hands. Then I knew creation's wait of eager expectation was over, that it had been liberated from its bondage to decay and brought into the glorious freedom of the children of God.

Suddenly, most glorious of all, I heard the rich, deep voice of the One beside me, begin to sing: "*Now the dwelling of God is with men, and I will live with them. They will be my people, and I myself will be with them and be their God. I will wipe every tear from their eyes. There will be no more death or mourning or crying or pain, for the old order of things has passed away. Behold, I am making everything new!*"

Redeeming the Time, Counting the Days

The infant: Oblivious, ignorant of the years, let alone the days, having no thought or concept of time.

The child: Simply enjoying the countless days of childhood — happy days, sad days, sometimes even bad days. Years marked by birthdays but having no awareness of the impact or import of days being passed, no time, or reason, to pause and notice their passing.

The adolescent: Counting the weeks, then days to birthdays, school holidays. Perhaps totting up the weeks of romantic relationship, days to exam results, hours to the end of the school day, minutes till the bell goes. Maybe penning the days in a diary, preserving them — for when, if ever? Never conscious though of days wasted — there's plenty more to come! What matters if an hour, a day is fritted away, there are so many — just waiting for tomorrow, to take their place.

The adult: Allotting years to study, months to a project, days to an assignment, hours to a task. Clocking in, signing in and signing up. Time: an entity to procrastinate over, prolong, anticipate, calculate, waste, discount, estimate, predict, postpone, delay, stretch out, forecast, vacillate about, hazard, gamble with, crumple up and throw away, try to recoup, make up for.

The parent: Counting the months, then weeks of pregnancy, wishing away the hours of confinement or the pangs of childbirth moments. Treasuring that first time of taking a child into their arms, followed by concerns of the days, the months, the years, the lifetime that lie ahead of them — as they watch over them, asleep, unconcerned and unaware. In the coming days, they record and rejoice over key moments, delight in their happiness, celebrate their achievements, mourn their sorrow and pain — and wonder. What are they thinking? What are they aware of? Do they know the clock is ticking?

The middle-aged: Time begins to fly. Where has the day gone? That's an hour wasted! It has taken me longer than it should have. The realisation that '*there is a time* for everything and a *season for every activity under the heavens*: a *time* to be born and a *time* to die'. The knowledge that: '*there is a tide in the affairs of men. Which, taken at the flood, leads on to fortune; omitted, all the voyage of their life is bound in shallows and in miseries. On such a full sea are we now afloat, and we must take the current when it serves, or lose our ventures*'.

The senior citizen: A counting of days; regretting times; recalling events; resuscitating memories; revisiting days; recapturing moments — dwelling on them, futilely trying to relive them. There is time to do this, all the time in the world for the time being, this moment, this instance. Questioning whether this time next year, there will be the possibility to ponder, to appreciate. Next Spring, will there be the chance to ask: '*What is this life if, full of care, we have no time to stand and stare? Or, no time to stand beneath the boughs and stare as long as sheep or cows?*' A calling to mind of chances not taken, opportunities missed, possibilities carelessly disregarded, occasions lost —stillborn.

The departed: In their passing, others recount their days (and their ways), making mention of some they valued, maybe regretted, felt sorrow over. Years of dedication and commitment acknowledged — even venerated, honoured, esteemed, respected, valued, prized and praised. But then — days die, the weeks and months are forgotten, till eventually, even the years, lapse into oblivion. Is there though, a place beyond, outside of time, where deceased lives, years, months, weeks, days, hours, minutes and even seconds, can be revived to live again? Is there some vast repository, where every moment, every action, every word, every thought is eternally stored? Only time will tell!

Thoughts of you, when looking back through Death's door

Child, thank you for walking with me to that dark door and seeing me safely through. As I looked back and saw you there, I thought of the many times we had walked together. Sometimes you used to skip, where before on shoulders I had carried you.

As you grew older, so did my love, my joy and my pride in you increase. I watched you, your beauty deepening yet ever constant. It is a great consolation for me to know, I have always been enthroned in your heart — never usurped. These thoughts of you have sustained me over the past weeks and months, as I sensed I was reaching that final door.

There was a time when the world considered I had given you away. But, you know you were too much a part of me, for that to be possible. So now, be comforted to know, I am so much a part of you, you could not have given me away to death.

I did not want to go but knew I must. It was only my love and my joy for you, my pride in you, which made it bearable. Too, it was the knowledge that we are bound together so tightly, even death cannot separate us.

You have never doubted in the past, when we were physically apart, that I was still there for you — so do not doubt it now. Whenever you feel we are apart, just think of me being there for you and sense me — out of sight but still in your heart.

Trying to bring forth fruit without the root

Change is often challenging and sometimes far from easy, especially when it comes to changing our attitudes and even more so when it comes to changing aspects of our character. It is all too easy and perhaps understandable, to respond negatively to things we find difficult to cope with, such as sorrow and yet, even sorrow can have a positive outcome. In this regard, some years ago, I found the following quote, from Mary Cholmondeley, a great encouragement: 'Sorrow with his pick mines the heart, but he is a cunning workman. He deepens the channels whereby happiness may enter, and he hollows out new chambers for joy to abide in, when he is gone'.

It may not answer all our questions but it does encourage us to believe that something beautiful may metamorphose from the ugliest of situations. Sometimes I am too quick to try and escape situations which cause me sorrow and don't allow the 'cunning workman' to complete his task. Perhaps this is one example of where I need to change my response. But, this is easier said than done!

The story is told of a young woman, who was struggling with her habit of responding negatively to sorrow. When she asked an older friend why that was, perceptively, the friend said, "You respond negatively to sorrow because the roots of life are in yourself. You are saying, 'Though I try I can't'. You are trying, instead of trusting. You are trying to bring forth fruit without the root." That suggests to me that there may be attitudes, attributes, characteristics that we can't change, it's just not in us.

Christians believe that Jesus is, as he claimed, the true vine and they are the branches. *'Without me'*, Jesus said, *'You can do nothing.'* In other words you can't bear fruit. For a branch to bear fruit, it needs to be connected to the vine. No root — no fruit. So, the choice is yours: try or trust. If you try to change and you succeed — great. If you don't succeed, try trusting — you never know.

A Shepherd's Tale

It was many years ago, but I remember it clearly, as though it was yesterday. I was living in Bethlehem, and it was only my third time being out watching the sheep at night. Of course, I had looked after the flock many times during the day, but night time was something different. Above all else, it was the stars.

Out on the hillside, away from the village, you had an uninterrupted view of the heavens, and they were magnificent. There were myriads of stars. I was reminded of what the Rabbi had taught us at the Synagogue, from the Psalms of David: *When I consider your heavens, the work of your fingers, the moon and the stars, which you have set in place, what is man that you are mindful of him, the son of man that you care for him.*

Anyway, I am forgetting myself, which I seem to do a lot nowadays. As I said, it was my third night, under the stars so to speak. I was just twelve and feeling very grown up. There was my father, Reuben; his brother Abel and his son, my older cousin Ezra, but they were all snoring quietly, as it was my turn to keep watch. There was no other sound, except the occasional bleat of a lamb or an owl calling.

I was just thinking of throwing another branch on the fire, when there was a blinding flash of light. I immediately closed my eyes. When I opened them again, and they became accustomed enough to see, I saw what I now know was an angel of the Lord, like the one which appeared to Gideon. At first, all I did was scream, as loud as I could, and turned to look at the others.

They all sprang to their feet immediately, but I could tell they were as terrified as I was. The angel obviously knew this, for he said, "Do not be afraid, I bring you good news of great joy that will be for all the people. Today in the town of David a Saviour has been born to you; he is Christ the Lord. This will be a sign to you: You will find a baby wrapped in cloths and lying in a manger."

His voice was very calming, but the effect only lasted for a second or two, before a great company of other angels appeared. It was as if every star in the sky had become an ange,l and the whole heavenly choir began to praise God, shouting out in unison, again and again: "Glory to God in the highest, and on earth peace to men on whom his favour rests."

It was breath taking. I fell to my knees and found myself shouting out the same words: "Glory to God in the highest, and on earth peace to men on whom his favour rests." As suddenly as it began, the shouts of the angels stopped, and, when I looked up, they were gone. Along with the others, I continued to shout out praises for a while. Suddenly there was silence, and overhead the stars seemed to shine more brightly, as though reflecting back the light of the angels.

With that, everyone began to talk at once. Gradually, things settled down, and my father said, "That was the most amazing thing I have ever seen. Let's go to Bethlehem, and see this thing that has happened, which the Lord has told us about." So, we hurried off back down into the town. We were so shocked and excited, we left the sheep and went to find this baby. Don't ask me how we found the stable, but it was next door to an inn. When I thought about it later, it was as though the Lord himself was whispering in our ear: "This is the way, walk in it!"

It was exactly as the angel had said. The baby was wrapped in cloths, and lying in a manger. His mother, who I later learned was called Mary, was kneeling down beside the manger, singing softly to the baby. She didn't look much older than me. A man, who I thought must be her husband, was standing alongside her, and even the ox and ass in the stable seemed to be looking on, as awestruck as we were.

No one said anything for a while, then I blurted out: "What's the baby's name?" The man, replied, "An angel appeared to me in a dream, and said I was to give him the name 'Jesus', because he will save his people from their sins." Mention of angels was enough for everyone to start sharing about what had happened out on the hillside. It was clear both Mary and her husband, were amazed at our story. Mary seemed especially moved by what we shared. I can't explain it but it was as though the words we spoke were dropping like seeds into her heart, and I knew, like me, she would remember the visit of the angels, and what they had said, long after it happened.

We hurriedly gave our apologies, and reluctantly left the little family. By then it was getting light, and people were beginning to come out of their houses, to start the day's chores. Of course, we were full of what had happened, and couldn't wait to let anyone and everyone know what we had seen and heard. Everyone we told, was amazed.

Eventually, Uncle Abel remembered the sheep. We made our way back up the hillside. All the way, we were glorifying and praising God, for all the things we had heard and seen, which were just as the angel had said.

Nearly sixty years have passed, but as I said, I remember that night, as if it were yesterday. What amazes me is that the angels appeared to us — mere shepherds. Most people see us as among the lowest of the low. Obviously, that can't be as Jesus sees us. Why do I say that? Well, some thirty or so years later, I was on a hillside, much like the one outside Bethlehem, when I heard that same Jesus say, "I am the Good Shepherd". I was instantly reminded of King David saying, "The Lord is my shepherd", and I repeated the same words to myself — "The Lord is my shepherd". The wonderful thing is that I know it is true — Jesus is my shepherd, and 'surely goodness and love will follow me all the days of my life, and I will dwell in the house of the Lord forever.'

What is God like?

I woke up one morning, with this question burning in my heart: 'What is God like?'

Immediately, the answer came: "What do you want me to be like?"

I found myself saying: "God, I want to know you love me."

Immediately, the answer came: "Just try speaking to Me, as though you wanted Me to love you."

So I did, saying : "God, I want to know You love me."

Immediately, I knew in my heart that He loved me.

Then, I found myself saying: "God, I want to know you understand me."

Immediately the answer came: "Just try speaking to Me, as though you wanted Me to understand you."

So I did, saying: "God I want to know You understand me."

Immediately, I knew in my heart that He understood me.

I was overwhelmed and said: "God, I want to know You forgive me."

Immediately, I knew in my heart He forgave me.

Then, I found myself asking: "God, are You everything I want you to be?"

Immediately, the answer came: "I am everything that is in accord with My nature."

So, I began to think of all the things I believed God to be.

Then, I found myself asking: "God, will You be my friend?"

Immediately, I knew in my heart He was my friend.

Then, I found myself saying: 'God, I want to know You are my Heavenly Father.'

Immediately, I knew in my heart, that He was my Heavenly Father.

And so it went on. Time and time again, He affirmed that He was who He was.

Now, thinking of you, reading this, I find myself asking God: "I want to know I can trust You to answer the questions anyone asks of You."

Immediately, the answer came back: "Peter, you know I've always answered you, whenever you've asked me anything, for that is in accord with My nature. Therefore you can trust Me, to do that for others.'

So my friend, no matter who you are, no matter where you are, no matter what you've done, I am confident that if you were to ask God to be like you want him to be, he will answer you.

It is that simple and uncomplicated. How do I know? Because I found myself asking, "God, I want to know You are so understandable, understanding and uncomplicated, that anyone can know You as their Heavenly Father."

Immediately, I knew in my heart, He was that understandable, understanding and uncomplicated.

But then, I found myself thinking, much though I love the thought that the little child in me can know God, I also wanted to know, he wanted the best for me. I wanted to know that he would challenge and encourage me. I wanted to know he would help me to reach my real potential and find my true purpose in life.

So, I found myself asking, "God, I want to know that You want the best for me. I want You to challenge and encourage me. I want to know You will help me to reach my true potential and to find my true purpose in life."

Immediately, I had my answer.

Why don't you discover for yourself what God is like? You can do this, by simply saying to him: "God, I want to know You what You are like."

Here is my last tip. Simply try saying: "God, I want to know You love me." That is His favourite! But so is: "God, I want to know You forgive me.' But whatever you ask, is His favourite question. You see that's the greatest secret of all, God truly is all you want Him to be – and more, much more!

I am amazing!

For you formed my inward parts; you knitted me together in my mother's womb. I praise you, for I am fearfully and wonderfully made. Wonderful are your works; my soul knows it very well. My frame was not hidden from you, when I was being made in secret, intricately woven in the depths of the earth. Your eyes saw my unformed substance; in your book were written, every one of them, the days that were formed for me, when as yet there was none of them. How precious to me are your thoughts, O God! How vast is the sum of them! If I would count them, they are more than the sand. I awake, and I am still with you.

Psalm 139:13-18

Doing an Internet search on something like: 'facts about the human body', you can come across some mind-boggling facts about the human body. Here are some I found, which blessed me. I have no way of personally verifying them, though most came from apparently reliable sources. From them I learned that I have been really busy today — in fact I have been every day of my life. Why do I claim that? Because, I understand that each day, I produce 170 billion red blood cells. I also produce another 230 billion other sorts of cells, during the same period. A blood cell can travel round my body in under twenty seconds, which means each one does so over 4,300 times a day. I wonder where I get all the energy from!

If that was not enough to do in a day, my heart beats over 100,000 times, pumping my blood through 62,000 miles of blood vessels (the equivalent of travelling two and a half times round the world at the equator). Daily, my heart produces enough energy to drive a truck twenty miles.

In the last four days, the lining of my stomach has been completely replaced, and happened at that rate throughout my life. I have also managed to get rid of a lot of weight today though? Why do I say that? Because I understand, some of the bacteria in my body can double every twenty minutes, and if my body had allowed them to do so, in a day they would weigh as much as Planet Earth.

Despite how many bacteria I kill off during the day, I still have to carry round an average of 32 million bacteria on every square inch of my body. Together, they make up 10% of my non-fluid body weight.

I have only just found out I am bioluminescent and glow in the dark. Apparently, the light that I emit is 1,000 times weaker than the human eyes are able to pick up, which is probably why I have lived so long without realising I glowed!

I read I use 17 muscles to smile but 43 to frown, so today, I decided to try and save my energy by smiling more than I frown!.

There are around 7,000,000,000,000,000,000,000,000,000 (7 octillion) atoms in my body. That is an estimate, as I have not had time to count them for a few days!

They say cold weather improves human memory and concentration. I must remember to stay out of the sun!

If I could manage to uncoil the DNA in all the cells in my body, I could stretch it from Earth to Pluto and back — ten billion miles!

In blinking one eye, I move two hundred muscles. When I blink, I shut my eyes for 0.3 seconds. If I saved up a life time's blinks for one blink, it would last fourteen months!

By the way, my eyes are the only known multi-focus lens, which can adjust within 2 milliseconds (two thousandths of a second). They have up to 120 million light-sensitive receptors, over 6 million colour-sensitive receptors, and over a million optic fibres, yet each eyeball is only 24.5 mm long. Little wonder I have to change the fluid that fills them, fifteen times a day!

The less-seen parts of my body are no less busy. Over my lifetime, my kidneys will have cleaned over 1 million gallons of blood. In each of my kidneys, there are a million filters, which clean over a litre of blood every minute, and produce nearly 1.5 litres of urine a day.

I do all this, without consciously thinking about it. Nevertheless, my brain is not idle! It is capable of thinking up more ideas than there are atoms in the universe, and its long-term memory can hold as much as a million billion (a quadrillion) separate pieces of information. It is a good job there are over 1,000,000,000,000,000 connections to enable it to do so. Little wonder, it can hold five times as much information, as the largest set of encyclopaedias.!

It is not as though, any part of my body is sitting around doing nothing. In just half an hour, it can produce enough energy to boil 2.25 litres of water. Mind you to do that, in the course of my life, I will consume around 7,000 times my body weight in food, spending five years doing so. It's a good job my large intestine is six feet long and the smaller intestine, a mere twenty one feet.

I have around thirty five billion white blood cells to fight against infective and foreign organisms, using 96,000 km of blood vessels to travel round my body. To enable this to happen, in a lifetime, my heart has to pump around a million barrels of blood — enough to fill two super tankers!

It wears me out, just thinking about all I have to do each day! In Psalm 139, King David, without the aid of the microscope, the telescope or the computer, showed he realised how fearfully and wonderfully he was made. How much more can I acknowledge the incredible, intricate skill with which my creator wove me and knitted me together.

(P.S. I stated I have no way of personally verifying the facts that I have shared above. This reminds me, that I cannot personally verify the accuracy or truth of most of what I hear or read. I just have to accept on trust and have a measure of healthy scepticism! Where I sense what I read or hear might have significance for me, as a Christian, I need to ask the Holy Spirit to show me whether it is true and reliable. In other words, I need to be discerning and *test the spirits*.)

Vision – Mission – Purpose

My vision, my mission, my purpose in life, remains to hear the Lord say, *"Well done thou good and faithful servant."* It is good though, from to time, to take stock of how things are in my walk with God.

The Past

There is nothing I can do about the past to change it, except to ask God for His forgiveness, to confess my sin to Him and accept that the sacrifice of Christ has cleansed me from all sin — every sin. I bitterly regret many of the things I have thought, said or done, which have grieved God and harmed others. But, I can only leave them all at the Cross. If there is anything of any worth in my past, God will allow it to be part of my legacy, for it is only through Him and by His grace that it has any worth.

The past is only of any value to me, if I have learnt from my mistakes and resolved to think, to say and to do differently. I can though allow all that I have experienced, have known of God's grace, to influence the present and the future — for good.

The Present

I believe The Lord has assigned my portion and my cup. He has made my lot secure. The boundary lines have fallen for me in pleasant places. Surely I have a delightful inheritance. I need to learn afresh, in whatsoever state I am, therewith to be content.

God is not bound by my sins, my mistakes, my failures, my limitations, my foibles, my nature, my character. There is nothing that disqualifies me from achieving God's purposes for my life. I claim the promise that there is now no condemnation to anyone who is in Christ and I am in Christ. I am a product of my past but I don't have to be its prisoner. I am also a product of His grace and what He has done in my life. I can therefore walk tall, exercising the wisdom of grace, knowing I am a child of God.

I accept that, so often, I have deviated from His purposes for my life. I believe there is little to be gained from a microscopic examination of the past, trying to decide where I went wrong. Rather I now need to do what the Lord requires of me: to act justly, to love mercy and to walk humbly with my God.

I need to focus on solutions. I need to regain control of my life, especially in regard to my thinking, my eating, my drinking AND my temper. I need to put to death what is earthly in me, especially being negative, being critical, begrudging giving to others. I need, as one of God's chosen ones, holy and beloved, to have a compassionate heart, to exercise kindness, humility, meekness, patience and gentleness and above all else, to express the love of God to everyone I come into contact with.

I can best do this by thinking, dwelling, meditating on what is honourable, just, pure, lovely, commendable, worthy of praise. I need to prize such things above the entertainment offered by the world. I need to change my viewing and listening habits.

In this way I can get back on track, I can realign my life with God's purposes for me. Accordingly, I recommit my life in its entirety, my time, my talents, my possessions, all that I am and have, to the Lord. I rededicate my life to Him, to have His own way, that His will might be done in me and through me.

The Future

As I seek to be solution-focused, God-focused, I can face the future, eternity, with confidence. I can be sure that God will make me part of His story and, by His grace, I can leave a legacy.

Whenever it feels time to do so, we should ask God to help us take stock. I find a good way of doing so, is by praying Psalm 139:

> *You have searched me, LORD, and you know me. You know*
> *when I sit and when I rise; you perceive my thoughts from*
> *afar. You discern my going out and my lying down; you are*

familiar with all my ways. Before a word is on my tongue you, LORD, know it completely. You hem me in behind and before, and you lay your hand upon me. Such knowledge is too wonderful for me, too lofty for me to attain.

Where can I go from your Spirit? Where can I flee from your presence? If I go up to the heavens, you are there; if I make my bed in the depths, you are there. If I rise on the wings of the dawn, if I settle on the far side of the sea, even there your hand will guide me, your right hand will hold me fast. If I say, "Surely the darkness will hide me and the light become night around me," even the darkness will not be dark to you; the night will shine like the day, for darkness is as light to you.

For you created my inmost being; you knit me together in my mother's womb. I praise you because I am fearfully and wonderfully made; your works are wonderful, I know that full well. My frame was not hidden from you when I was made in the secret place, when I was woven together in the depths of the earth. Your eyes saw my unformed body; all the days ordained for me were written in your book before one of them came to be.

How precious to me are your thoughts, God! How vast is the sum of them! Were I to count them, they would outnumber the grains of sand— when I awake, I am still with you.

Search me, God, and know my heart; test me and know my anxious thoughts. See if there is any offensive way in me, and lead me in the way everlasting.

THE PRINCESS FOREVER-FOREVER

A magic fairy story for daughters who have nearly forgotten who they are.

This is a magic story, a magic kind of magic, which only those who have never completely grown up inside can understand. Part of the magic is that, every daughter who reads it, can start to believe she is the little girl the story is all about. The story is also about a foolish king, and begins as every good fairy story begins.

Once upon a time in Fairyland (where everyone lives at some time or other), there lived a king. The king (like all kings) had lots of names, one of the king's names was **'THE KING FOREVER-FOREVER'** but his magic name (which only a very privileged few could call him) was **'DADDY'**. At times, he wasn't a very clever king (but then you don't have to be clever to be a king in Fairyland).

Although he wasn't always very clever, he always tried to be kind and loving, **AND** he could always do lots and lots of magic things (that is when he wanted to, and when he remembered). Now the king had a daughter, whom he naturally loved very much. I can't tell you all her names, because she had so many, but I'll tell you two of them. One of them is the same as yours, and the other is **'THE PRINCESS FOREVER-FOREVER'**, which is the name we'll use for this story.

Every day (well nearly every day because as I forgot to tell you — the king used to forget things); nearly every day the king would do magic things for the princess. Some days it seemed he would do magic things everywhere and all the time. Sometimes it was 'FUN MAGIC', which made you laugh and laugh, till you almost cried. I don't think it would have been good for you, if it had been that sort of magic all day and every day though–it would have worn you out.

On other days, and sometimes on the same days, the magic that the king did was an extra lovely kind of magic — 'CUDDLE MAGIC', which cuddled you till you were lovely and warm, from the inside out. But always it was such a special magic, which only princesses can experience (which was why it was so special).

The king was often very busy doing things that only kings seem to know needed doing (which, incidentally, no one else except the king saw being done), but which he always did (though no one else noticed they'd been done). It was because he was so busy that sometimes he forgot to do magic things. When he did remember though, the magic he did, helped the princess forget the times when he forgot.

At the time our story begins, the princess was seven years old, which you'll remember from when you were seven, is the time when kings can do their best magic. When the princess was seven, she thought her father, the king (or should I say 'Daddy'), was the most magic person there had ever been.

Oh — but now I'm forgetting. I forgot to tell you this is a sad story. Perhaps if I'd told you that at the beginning though, you wouldn't have started to read it. **BUT** don't forget this is a magic story too, a magic kind of magic, which always makes a sad story have a happy ending. This makes you wonder whether it was ever really sad in the first place (even though in places it may make you cry), especially when you remember how very unhappy it was sometimes.

One of the things which the king forgot to tell the princess was why he **COULD DO** magic things, and why he **DID** them. As I've remembered now (for I did forget), I'll tell you. It was simply, because the princess was his daughter, **FOREVER**, and that he was The King Forever-Forever, he could do any magic things at all, and it was also the reason why he did them. As long as they both remembered who they were, the king could do the magic things, which were so often invisible to anyone but the princess herself.

I was forgetting too, that by now, the magic of this story (the magic kind of magic that I told you about), will have started to work. You will have begun to change into The Princess Forever-Forever (although you may not have realised that yet). As you are changing into The Princess Forever-Forever, you may have started to forget things. The reason for this is that you are the daughter **FOREVER** of The King Forever-Forever, who sometimes forgets things — even the most important things of all. But remember, **PLEASE, PLEASE REMEMBER**, you're The Princess Forever-Forever, which (because the magic of this story is so strong) **YOU ALWAYS HAVE BEEN — FOREVER.**

Let me tell you though, what happened when the princess was seven, and, though it makes you sad, remember there's a happy ending (and it's also a fairy story and all real fairy stories come true). At that time, her father, the king, did the most silly, the most unmagic thing a king can do. He tried to make himself forget that he was The King Forever-Forever, even though as I've said it was at the time when kings can do their best magic. I won't tell you now why he did it but (at the time) he thought that it was the right thing to do. You remember of course that (though he always tried to be kind and loving), at times he wasn't very clever and forgot things and this was one of those times. What he didn't remember is, if , only for a moment, you stop living up to your name as 'Daddy', your magic is never so good.

At the same time as the king tried to make himself forget he was The King Forever-Forever, he told his daughter, he would be going away, and she may not see him again for a long time. Although she didn't know her father was trying to make himself forget that he was The King Forever-Forever, she still knew enough to be very sad.

When the king left and he was out of sight, he took off his crown (which he'd always worn—even on those days when he forgot to do magic things). While he had been wearing the crown, which was made of gold and precious stones, it hadn't seemed to weigh anything at all (which was all part of the magic that went with being The King Forever-Forever). He put the crown in a black bag, which he carried with him wherever he went, from that day on. He tried so hard to make himself forget he was The King Forever-Forever, he eventually forgot what was in the heavy bag he was carrying — even though it was so heavy it made his heart hurt.

Meanwhile, the princess (who was left wondering what her father had meant) grew sadder and sadder. Although other people around could do some magic things, they were never the same or as good as the magic things her father, the king, had done. One very important thing happened though. The princess found a magic picture that the king (without realising it) had left behind. Of course, you will understand that it was invisible to anyone but the princess herself, as it was a magic picture. Yet even she didn't know how the magic worked.

When she first found the magic picture, she could see everything in it very clearly. It was a picture of herself, with the king, her father, standing beside her. He had his arm round her, looking very proud. At the bottom, in beautifully written letters, it said, 'The King Forever-Forever and his daughter The Princess Forever-Forever'. I don't think she would have known what to do, if she hadn't found that picture (even though it made her very sad to look at it and she couldn't talk to anyone else about it).

One of the saddest things of all is that (because it was a magic picture, which he had painted before he tried to make himself forget who he was), the longer the king was away, the fainter the picture became. If this hasn't happened to you, you would find it hard to believe. The first thing that happened was the writing got fainter. Next, the king became shadowy too. Eventually, the writing disappeared completely and so did the image of the king. When this happened, the princess found she couldn't remember what the king had looked like, and (although she never completely forgot the magic things he did) she began to forget that she was The Princess Forever-Forever. Worse still, she tried to make herself forget she was a princess at all.

I did promise you though, this won't be a sad story in the end, though it was very sad for many years. Although the king almost forgot that he was The King Forever-Forever, he never completely forgot his daughter (though you may find that hard to believe, when he'd almost forgotten who **HE** was).

A long time passed, many years in fact. The first years were the longest and, because they were the longest, they were also the saddest. Whenever she was on her own and missing the magic, the princess would get out the picture and try desperately to remember how it had been. When she looked at it hard enough, she could remember there had been someone standing beside her. The strange thing was, a tiny part of her remembered who it was, although she'd almost completely forgotten.

Gradually it seemed to her, even the picture of herself changed and she didn't like herself so much. She started to think that somehow she was to blame, because the picture seemed so empty, and not as lovely as it had been. With the writing gone, she no longer saw herself for who she was–The Princess Forever-Forever. Instead, she painted different pictures of herself — which somehow looked more like how she felt. Although they looked nothing like her, she began to believe they did. She decided it was no longer her in the magic picture and she began to feel a misfit and sadly even a freak. After a time, it seemed to her she was out of place, wherever she was. and this made her very unhappy at times.

Meanwhile the king continued on his travels. I know he would have found life totally unbearable, if he'd known how his daughter saw herself. Although he did lots of magic things for other children, whom he grew to love very much, he could never deep down, forget the magic things he had once done for the princess. When he thought about her, the heavy sack on his back made his heart hurt even more.

Well, that would have been how the story ended, if it wasn't a magic story, a magic kind of magic which makes even a sad story have a happy ending. At the time when the king and the princess were as far away from remembering who they really were, as they could be, a beautiful new magic began to work. It started when the princess herself gave birth to a baby boy. Although from the start, she loved him for himself, it was as though his coming began to speak to her of how things still should have been for her. As her little boy grew, she found she could do magic things for him (this was because she'd never stopped being the daughter of The King Forever-Forever). Perhaps it was in discovering she could do magic things for her son, she remembered how magic things had been done for her.

One day, she found herself looking at her son, and remembering the magic picture. Quickly she found it, and the magic of the picture began to work. In her mind's eye, she saw herself standing before the door of a lovely little house, which looked as though it had been closed up for a long time. She found herself wondering, whether anyone still lived there. She imagined knocking at the door, but no one answering. She imagined trying the door, finding it was locked though.

Something told her, the photo was the key to unlocking the door. She saw again, where the king, her father, had been, and it seemed as though a shadowy picture of a man began to appear again. She started to realise he was someone who was very special to her, and she knew she must find him. As the days went by (although the picture of the king was no clearer), the princess became more determined to find him.

She hardly dared hoped she would find him, and certainly she could never begin to believe he might still want to do magic things for her. After all she thought, I'm not a princess now — though you know, she was **STILL** The Princess Forever-Forever. Nevertheless, you'll have guessed, she did set out to find him. At first, it seemed a very difficult task, and she didn't feel she could ask anyone she knew for help (in case they laughed at her or were unkind). Even so, she became more and more sure that she should do it.

Although it was very difficult to find him, and she had to search for a long time, and in the strangest places — suddenly, one magic day, she found him. When she had almost given up hope, she found herself at the door of that little locked up house. Although she couldn't be sure, she felt this was where her search would end. Suddenly, she noticed a beautifully shaped knocker. What she didn't know was that this was a magic knocker, which only she could have seen. Bravely (for her heart was trembling a lot), she knocked at the door.

The king, who was inside, heard the knocking, but (although he'd been waiting for so long to hear it) he had forgotten that only the princess could have discovered the knocker. Nevertheless, he went to see who was there. Eventually he found the key that was hanging by the door (covered in cobwebs of forgetfulness). It took him a little while to unlock the door, and it creaked a lot as he opened it. When he did so though, he found the most beautiful young woman standing there.

When she saw him, she felt so happy and sad, at one and the same time, she was sure her head and heart would burst. When her father saw her, his heart felt as though it would burst too, and he hardly knew what to do. The tears began to roll down his cheeks, he dropped the sack (which he'd always carried with him wherever he was), and out fell his crown. Up to that moment, both of them had still forgotten who they really were. Indeed, if it hadn't been for the magic picture the princess had brought with her, they may not have discovered the truth as quickly as they did.

When the princess showed her father the magic picture, the most wonderful, the most magical thing happened. The picture of the king and his daughter had become as clear as crystal, and almost seemed alive, it was so real. Underneath the picture, as it had always been (though the princess hadn't been able to see it again till now), in beautifully written letters it read: 'The King Forever-Forever and his daughter The Princess Forever-Forever'.

The king still couldn't believe it, although his heart was filled with such a deep joy, mixed with sadness. He felt he couldn't look at the princess, because he was so overwhelmed with love for her, and yet felt so ashamed, as he realised how silly and unmagical a thing he'd done all that time ago. The princess suddenly remembered the crown, which was lying at her feet. She knew what she must do. With great care, she lifted the heavy crown, and reached up to place it on her father's bowed head. At that moment, they both began to remember who they really were.

Suddenly, the king found himself doing magic again. First it was the 'fun magic', which made the princess laugh and laugh, till she almost cried. Then wonderfully, when she felt she couldn't take any more, the king started to do that lovely kind of magic, which cuddled the princess, till she was lovely and warm from the inside out. Though she was now much older and more grown up on the outside, the princess realised how much she had missed that 'cuddle magic', and how much she still needed it.

The reason for this was that on the inside, there was still part of her which would always be only seven years old, and that seven year old little girl, was always desperate for the 'cuddle magic', which only her daddy could do.

So it was (even though they hardly dared to), they began to believe that they really were 'The King Forever-Forever and his daughter The Princess Forever-Forever, which of course they always had been. From that moment on, they started to discover again, just what that meant. The days to come would be full of magic, as they found what they thought they'd lost forever.

I'm sure you've guessed that they lived happily ever after, because this is a magic story and all magic stories have a happy ending — it's also a fairy story and all real fairy stories come true.

SO REMEMBER, PLEASE, PLEASE REMEMBER (NO MATTER HOW LONG HE'S BEEN GONE OR HOW SILLY AND FORGETFUL TO DO MAGIC HE'S BEEN) YOUR FATHER IS STILL 'THE KING FOREVER-FOREVER' AND YOU'LL ALWAYS BE 'THE PRINCESS FOREVER-FOREVER' – FOREVER.

Some Estimations!!!

There are 100 trillion (1 followed by 14 noughts–100,000,000,000,000) cells in one human body. It is estimated that 50,000 of these cells die and are replaced every three seconds.

There are 2 quadrillion (2 followed by 15 noughts–2,000,000,000,000,000) bacterial cells in one human body. Some of these bacteria can double in number every twenty minutes. Growing unchecked, in a day, such a single bacterium, doubling every twenty minutes, could turn into 5 million quadrillion (5 followed by 21 noughts–5,000,000,000,000,000,000,000) bacteria. This is roughly the weight of the earth in tons.

It would take 3,500 years to count the 200 to 400 billion stars in the Milky Way at the rate of one per second. It is thought, there may be as many as 125 billion galaxies in the universe. One recent estimate is that there are 70 sextillion (7 followed by 22 noughts–70,000,000,000,000,000,000,000) stars in the universe.

If Earth equalled the size of a golf ball, then the Sun would be 15 feet in diameter. You could fit 960,000 Earths into the Sun.

If Earth equalled the size of a golf ball, then the star Betelgeuse would be SIX TIMES the Empire State Building (6 x 1,250 = 7,500 feet). You could fit 262 trillion (262 followed by twelve noughts = 262,000,000,000,000) Earths into Betelgeuse.

If Earth equalled the size of a golf ball, then the star Mu Cephei would be twice the Golden Gate Bridge wide i.e. 3.5 miles. You could fit 2.7 quadrillion earths (2,700 followed fifteen noughts = 2,700,000,000,000,000,000.) Earths into Mu Cephei.

If Earth equalled the size of a golf ball then the star Carnis Majorus would be the height of Mount Everest wide 30,000 feet i.e. 5.5 miles. You could fit 7 quadrillion earths (7 followed eighteen noughts = 7,000,000,000,000,000,000.) Earths into Carnis Majorus.

It is estimated that there are 300 billion stars in the Whirlpool Galaxy, which is 31,000,000 light years away. One light year = 5.88 trillion miles (5,880,000,000,000 miles), therefore the Whirlpool Galaxy is 182,280,000,000,000,000,000 miles away.

(Authors Note: Again I can not personally verify these facts. Some of them came from the Readers Digest, many years ago. Others are from Louis Giglio. I am a real fan of his and particularly enjoy his videos, especially ones like '*How great is our God*', where many of these facts were taken from.)

Appreciation

Whilst in China, coming up the subway onto Tianamen Square, I saw a mother and father with their daughter of about eight. I was struck, by seeing the obvious appreciation of the parents for her, the specialness of the child in their eyes. I was reminded of the following thoughts I had recorded, on watching an Afro-Caribbean couple with their little daughter aged 6-9 months, in an Indian restaurant in Bradford, England some years ago.

Whatever age your children are, appreciate them, and enjoy them to the full. The riches you gain, by treasuring each fleeting moment, will increase the bounty, which every parent can amass. As you do so, you will discover that the joy of being a parent, is not limited to the span of their childhood. Rather it extends to the length of your life, for continually appreciating your child, will enrich your life, providing you with poignant pleasures, which few experiences can surpass.

Your appreciation of them will be a strong defence, which will protect them in the emotional, relational and social battles of life. This will mean, even if they become a casualty or surrender to the pressures, going under, causing you heartache, you can continue to appreciate them. Diamonds are formed, when carbon is subjected to intense heat and pressure but often the diamond, which is a child can go undiscovered, because no one ever looked for them.

Value your child for who they are, not by what they have done or failed to do. If you do so, it could prove to be a lifeline for them, and a key for you to unlock further treasures for yourself. Remember, no matter how old they are, no matter how age, circumstances or even denial try to disguise it, they will still be a child — a child who needs to be appreciated. When you appreciate your child, remember to appreciate the little child that lives within you — even if you are the oldest of people. When we give the gift of appreciation to our children, we should also give it to ourselves. When we sow a seed of appreciation, we reap a harvest of delight. When we fail to appreciate a child, fields, which could be full of joy, lie fallow.

A Father's Touch

Some years ago, I was travelling back home to Norfolk, after spending a few days in my home city of London. Driving along, I was very much aware of an area in my life, where I was experiencing continual failure, and which had been especially problematic during my time away.
I felt God start to show me why the Enemy homed in on this area of my life, as he did with so many other men. As a consequence of this, I found myself praising God aloud. Before I knew it, I was shouting out my praises, glad that no one else was in the car, to know what a noise I was making.

This continued for some miles, by which time I was quite hoarse. I then asked God (for the umpteenth time). to forgive me for this particular sin. I was immediately overwhelmed, by my own unworthiness and God's acceptance and forgiveness. Consequently, I alternated between sorrowful remorse and contented joy, laughter and crying. As I laughed, the tears ran down my cheeks.

I had reached the last town before home, about six miles away, and was still driving along, when I saw myself in heaven, approaching the throne of God. As I walked towards His throne, I could see to either side of me, there were ranks of angels seated — watching me. It was rather like the people in the stands, watching a great celebration, like the Coronation of The Queen in Westminster Abbey. In my hands, I was carrying something black, slimy, organic, seemingly alive. I bent down, and placed it before God. I knew it was this particular sinful activity.

Instantly, God reached down and touched it. Immediately, it was transformed into a shining, golden vessel, and I heard my Heavenly Father say: "Look what my son's brought me". I found myself protesting to the angels, it wasn't what I had brought Him, but I knew it was. The realisation dawned that, even if I failed again in this area, there was nothing the Devil could do, which could reverse what God had done. The moment God's touch had transformed my offering, it meant it could never be destroyed, its eternal existence was assured.

Suddenly, I began to laugh, like I'd never laughed before. It was deep laughter, which welled up from my stomach. It was so different to any laughter I had ever known before and it was so cathartic. My insides ached and I cried out to God to stop it, though I wanted it to last forever. I was laughing so much, and couldn't stop, so that when I reached the junction where I needed to turn left, to make my way home, I had to keep going straight on. I knew my in-laws would be there visiting, and I was in no state for them to see me. The front of my shirt was drenched with tears and I just couldn't stop laughing.

All I could do was to keep going along the main road, to the next town, about five miles further on. From there, I made my way home by the coast road. By the time I pulled up outside my home, I had calmed down enough to show my face.

I feel so privileged to have had such a wonderful and dramatic experience of God's grace, but I hesitate to share it, in case people think I am boasting, making out I am special. In my heart of hearts though, I know God delights to give such experiences to anyone who's desperate enough to abandon themselves to His grace and mercy.

What do I believe?

Jesus said: "*I am . . . . the truth.*" John 14:6. For truth to be meaningful, for it to impact and affect us, it must essentially be simple and yet sophisticated. Simple, defined as being: Easily understood or done; presenting no difficulty; plain, basic, or uncomplicated in form, nature, or design (Oxford Dictionaries). Sophisticated, defined as: Having, revealing, or involving a great deal of worldly experience and knowledge of fashion and culture; of a person or their thoughts, reactions and understanding, aware of and able to interpret complex issues; subtle (Oxford Dictionaries).

I want to try and decide what I believe about God and why. I do not intend attempting a philosophical analysis, or writing a theological discourse — for I could do neither. I cannot believe either will provide me with a foundation for my beliefs. Whatever truth there is to know, it cannot be subject of a person's intellect. If God is the god I believe Him to be, then He will have made it possible for everyone to know Him. The simplest soul to the most intellectual, must be able to discover what they need to know about Him. Romans 1 : 19-20 sums this up for me: '*For what can be known about God is plain to them, because God has shown it to them. For his invisible attributes, namely, his eternal power and divine nature, have been clearly perceived, ever since the creation of the world, in the things that have been made. So they are without excuse*'.

I therefore accept that my beliefs will be based on subjective understanding and acceptance, rather than objective reasoning. This means, I could never really prove anything I believe to another. Ultimately, in regard to their beliefs, everyone lives by faith — no one can objectively prove anything in relation to their personal beliefs.

I believe that God has always existed, He was before Time, outside of Time — He is eternal. He is outside of Space — He is infinite and He is everywhere — *in him we live and move and have our being* Acts 17:28. I cannot believe otherwise. If He is eternal and infinite, my mind cannot comprehend that. God is far greater than I could ever imagine or think. It would be utterly impossible to believe that I could condense God to a size I could understand.

Theology has been defined, as a study of the nature of God and religious belief. It could be argued that, to attempt to reduce God in this way, to a being that can be rationally understood or proven, is completely futile. I am told, the Sun is 94 million miles away, and that the light from the sun takes 8 minutes to reach earth. This means, it travels at 705,000,000 miles an hour. I am also told, in one second, the Sun releases power enough to provide the energy needs of the world for 500,000 years. AND the Sun is only an average star, in an average galaxy! I cannot truly comprehend those facts, so how can I hope to definitely know anything of any significance about the One who "created the heavens and the earth and all things visible and invisible" — except it is by revelation. Revelation can only come from outside oneself.

Revelation can be defined as God supernaturally revealing the truth about Himself, in a way which we would otherwise not be able to discover for ourselves or otherwise know. I understand the word 'revelation', is either of two Greek words *phanerosis* and *apokalupsis*. *Phanerosis* means to make something known, to reveal something to another, to make it visible or clear. The root word is *phos*, meaning 'light'. In order for anything to be revealed, there must be light and the source of that light is God himself.

So, if I understand correctly, *phanerosis* refers to something that is physically made visible – a manifestation. Therefore for revelation as *phanerosis* to be complete, something needs to be experienced at first hand. It follows too, that I need to think of revelation in terms of *apokalupsis,* meaning a supernatural unveiling or disclosure of a truth, like the unveiling of a statue.

Today, we put great store on human reasoning and scientific research, but these could never be the means by which we, as individuals, can learn more of the nature of God — especially if, primarily, God reveals himself through revelation. In any case, as I have suggested previously, the capacity for the depth of logical reasoning or scientific experiment otherwise needed, is beyond all but the most intellectual and erudite. No, what we learn of God, must be what he chooses to supernaturally reveal to us. As Jesus said: *'No one knows the Father except the Son and anyone to whom the Son chooses to reveal him.' (Matthew 11:27).* God alone,

Father, Son and Spirit, is the well-spring from which I must drink, if I am to imbibe the living water that will refresh my soul and spirit.

I digress for a while to look at theology. In his classic work on theology 'In understanding be men' T C Hammond wrote: *'It is necessary . . . . . to learn that there will always remain unavoidable gaps in every theological system. Where divine Revelation has not pointed the way it is extremely unwise for human speculative philosophy to attempt to do so. When a classification has been extended to a point where (in any particular) it cannot claim the authority of Scripture, it has ceased to be useful and is rapidly becoming a danger. Reverent agnosticism is preferable to unauthorised speculation.'*

I am certain I am not an agnostic (someone who believes that nothing is known or can be known of the existence or nature of God), but the mention of *every theological system*, evidences that no one system of theology can claim to be absolute truth, absolutely right. Every system, will be limited by the subjectivity of those who devised it, and those who use it as a basis for their beliefs. I am, however, not decrying theology, it has great value.

If ultimately though, everything I (we) believe is dependent on revelation, why do we need theology. Could it be that we always need to have an answer, an objective hook on which to hang our beliefs? Can we only be satisfied, if we can prove something, to claim that we are right, that we have a monopoly of truth? Do we feel insecure, if we feel we have not got an answer for others, which will stand up to objective investigation? Do we feel that others need to be able to acknowledge our objectivity – even if they do not share our interpretation?

Could it be too, that we, a group, a community, need to have a set of basic beliefs, which can be used, consciously, subconsciously or unconsciously, deliberately or unwittingly, to control that group or community. Is it like at the start of a training course, where the trainer gets participants to agree on a set of ground rules, to facilitate proceedings. Ultimately, this enables him or her (hopefully for the best of reasons) to control things, to ensure that things run smoothly. Without such an agreed "creed", things could get out of hand, therefore it is necessary to have something which is inviolable, cannot be questioned.

In the context of a training course, having a set of ground rules, is clearly of great benefit, but is such a statement of basic beliefs, of fundamental importance within a church setting? Clearly, it has benefit in helping people, when they are thinking of joining a group, to decide whether they broadly agree with the beliefs held within the group. Equally clearly, it is decidedly unhelpful, indeed harmful, where it is used as a means to prevent, discourage or disallow people to question anything, with the threat of being 'excommunicated', if you do so.

I have always believed and have been told in church groups and by speakers and preachers, that God is not thrown by our questions, that his throne is not rocked, his authority is not threatened. We need to let Him know honestly, how we feel, not because He needs to know but rather we need to know, that He knows how we feel. We should therefore feel able to question everything —appropriately, courteously and reverently, within a church fellowship, where everyone's views and questions are valued and accepted as equally valid.

I came across the following quote which suggests that, as an individual, I need to examine everything I hear, read, have heard, have read, and hold it up to scripture and allow the Holy Spirit to reveal the truth: *Among the gifts of the Spirit scarcely one is of greater practical usefulness than the gift of discernment. This gift should be highly valued and frankly sought as being almost indispensable in these critical times. This gift will enable us to distinguish the chaff from the wheat and to divide the manifestations of the flesh from the operations of the Spirit.* (A W Tozer)

Whenever anyone shares anything which concerns our beliefs as Christians, we need to subject what they say to critical examination. To do this, we should be like the Bereans (mentioned in Acts 17:11). We read of them: *Now the Bereans were of more noble character than the Thessalonians, for they received the message with great eagerness and examined the Scriptures every day to see if what Paul said was true.* I am sure Paul was not thrown by this but rather he would have welcomed this exercise of discernment. I am certain too, he would have agreed with the Apostle John, who, in 1 John 4:1, says: *Dear friends, do not believe every spirit, but test the spirits to see whether they are from God, because many false prophets have gone out into the world.*

No matter how long we have been Christians, we need, from time to time, to remind ourselves of what we believe. Creeds such as the Nicene, the Apostles' or the Athanasian, have an important role in this respect, especially in corporate worship. Neglecting the use of them, as happens in many non-conformist gatherings, means groups of believers can go for many weeks, without touching on various doctrines, which we all need to be reminded of. An added benefit of saying creeds together, is the unifying effect they have, reminding us of what we share. However, on their own, they can be little more than *a resounding gong or a clanging cymbal.* Rather, we need to be bound with *cords which cannot be broken.* When we come together, we need to experience with each other, we need to feel: *faith, hope and love. But the greatest of these is love.*

As with the corporate, so it is with the individual. We need time alone with God, to remind us what we know and understand about him. We need to feel the *faith, hope and love,* which, ultimately, can only be found in him, because he has revealed himself as their source. But, the greatest of these is love, which can only be fully experienced, when we are as close as a child can possibly get to their father. God is not going to judge me on my theology, he is going to judge me on the basis of my love for Him and my response to His revelation of Himself. It is in this assurance I put my faith and this gives me the certainty of hope.

SNIPPETS

Achieving God's purposes

The three ingredients for individual optimum achievement are: Competence, Commitment and Confidence. If someone has proven their competence to a certain level, appropriate to the stage of development they are at, and shown their commitment to accomplish the challenge they now face, then they can have the confidence to believe they can achieve.

Those who love God, and desire to fulfil His purposes for their lives, have the added benefits of the gifts and abilities He has given them, coupled with the desire He has planted in their soul and spirit, to please Him. All that needs to be added, is the faith to believe that no purpose of His can be thwarted.

This potent mix of the natural and supernatural, means nothing is beyond the grasp of the man and woman of God, who wants to see God's will come to pass in their lives.

A Little Boy's Adventure!

It was a beautiful day, the sky having been turned a brilliant blue by the fast-fading reds and oranges of dawn. Just the day for an adventure. Looking down at the little boy beside him, the Lord said, "Take my hand, son; there's somewhere I want to take you". Eagerly, the boy took his hand and they set off. The air around them crackled with animated chatter, the high-pitched voice of the child and the Lord's strong, but gentle tone. There was much laughter, and the pace was as much a skip as a stroll.

At first, the boy took little notice of his surroundings. Rather, he kept sneaking up glances, to the Lord's face, as though needing to pinch himself, it was really happening. He was setting off on an adventure, with the bestest friend in the whole world. And, always it seemed, whenever he turned his face up to look, the Lord was smiling down at him, and yet there was a touch of sadness in his gaze, which as yet the boy did not notice.

"Where are we going?" asked the boy.

"Now, there's the mystery", said the Lord. "If I told you now, you would be none the wiser, for it's somewhere you've never been before. But, I've been there, and got everything ready, so I know you're going to like it — trust me!"

God's Low Whisper

All around me the world is crying out — cries of need and indifference; cries of anger, even of hatred; cries of intolerance and bigotry; cries of confusion, as well as bitterness. Each an expression of hurt or frustration, anguish or pain.

Joining the cacophony are the appeasing sounds of the principalities and powers of darkness, offering false hopes of relief. They are seeking to seduce, to deceive, to divert, to distract; doing anything they can to prevent me hearing the still, small voice, the low whisper of God. These demonic disruptors, realising how I need to hear God speak into my life, begin to shout the louder, trying to allure me, to get my attention.

Miraculously though, as I choose to block out all other sounds, human or diabolical, I hear the low whisper of God, speaking clearly into my situation. Softly, yet strongly, he speaks into my need, my indifference, my anger, my hatred, my intolerance, my bigotry, my confusion, my bitterness. Gently, the Balm of Gilead soothes my hurt, my frustration, my anguish, my pain; speaking in words of His love, His mercy, His truth, His healing, His joy, His peace, His comfort, His encouragement, His consolation, His freedom — He reliefs my distress. I realise I can hear nothing but His voice. I feel myself being renewed, restored, refreshed, reinvigorated, replenished; ready to speak these same comforts into the lives of others.

Can God get better?

A bit factious but I cannot resist asking the question: Can God get better? In Revelation 1:8, God says: "*I am the Alpha and the Omega*" – literally the beginning and the end. Whilst in Ecclesiastes 7:8 we read: *Better is the end of a thing than the beginning.* I guess the answer is God was only speaking figuratively in Revelation 1:8, as the verse in its entirety reads: *I am the Alpha and the Omega, says the Lord God, who is and who was and who is to come, the Almighty.* In other words, God is not only eternal, He is complete — God has no beginning or no end!

The Hebrew word for completeness, wholeness is 'Shalom'. I don't find it too difficult to believe God is complete. I have found him to be all that Strong's Concordance says of *Shalom — completeness, wholeness, health, peace, welfare, safety, soundness, tranquillity, prosperity, perfectness, fullness, rest, harmony, the absence of agitation or discord'.*

Jesus said, "I have come that they may have life, and have it to the full" — abundantly, completely, wholly. John 10:10(NIV — expanded). Clearly, God's plan, His purpose, is that we should enjoy 'Shalom', that we should be like Him.

Seeing in the dark

In the blackest of nights, when my eyes of faith could not penetrate the darkness, I could have believed that God was not there, that He had deserted me. Instead though, I chose to believe what He had said to me, 'I will not leave you or forsake you; I will always be there with you.'

As I stood in the silence of the night, I felt my desire for His presence growing within me. I began to appreciate how God could be working the darkness together for good, as my longing for Him increased.

Strangely, the darkness became less threatening, as the light of under-standing began to dawn. Gradually, I found myself seeing in the dark. Just as, *the City needed neither lamp nor the sun, as God was its light*, so too, neither did I. In the stillness, I could sense the Lord's presence, and thought I heard the sound of his breathing; He seemed that close.

Then, as suddenly as it was dawn, so as suddenly, it was dusk once more and the darkness closed in around me. But, I had seen enough!

Every day

Then he said to them all: "Whoever wants to be my disciple must deny themselves and take up *their cross* daily *and follow me."* Luke 9 v 23

An old hymn said:
The daily round, the common task, should furnish all we need to ask, Room to deny ourselves, a road to bring us daily nearer God.

Whatever happens in a day, no matter how mundane or ordinary, it is part of God's plan and purpose for me. I need to learn not to begrudge the opportunity to deny myself the time to do what I want. Instead, I need to welcome the opportunity to do the will of God, so showing myself to be a faithful servant.

Natural and Supernatural Mathematics

There is a law in Natural Mathematics which states that the product of zero, multiplied by any number, always equals zero. Therefore: $0 \times 6,473 = 0$.

Supernatural Mathematics teaches me that someone who apart from God can do nothing, multiplied by God, equals someone who can do all things through Christ.

Pithy Pieces

Carpe Diem? You cannot seize the day, but you can capture each moment of that day, and subject it to your control.

* * * *

In the realm of social dynamics, a catalyst is an individual who accelerates a social interaction, without being personally affected. One of the rules of therapy, is that a clinician should not become emotionally involved with someone they are trying to help (sometimes referred to as 'a client'). Ancient wisdom purports, it is impossible for someone to help a fellow human being, without being emotionally involved to some extent. Is such thinking superstitious and dangerous?

* * * *

The theorem of contentment states that in any right angled attitude, the square of the happiness equals the square of the other two sides, no matter how long they are.

* * * *

The theory of probability states that if you toss a negative thought, you have at least as much chance of it landing positive face up than not.

* * * *

To flush out an unhealthy cistern of thinking, irrigate the whole system with a constant flow of positivity.

* * * *

Christians believe that the relationship between the negative and positive is a key determinant in personal contentment and equilibrium. As it says in Ecclesiastes 7:18: *It is good to grasp the one and not let go of the other. Whoever fears God will avoid all extremes.*

* * * *

You determine your true state, not by how you were, nor by how you fear you might be but by how you are now. Notice the use of the stronger word 'determine' rather than the use of the weaker one 'decide'.

* * * *

People with high levels of negativity are more likely to be infected with despair, than those who inoculate themselves with enthusiasm.

* * * *

It is easier to maintain homeostasis by holding on to each end, rather than trying to balance, whilst not grasping either pole.

* * * *

In the realm of human relationships, experiential proof is more easily and soundly acquired by subjective sensing, than by objective reasoning.

* * * *

If you pour enough positive material into a black hole, it finally implodes and a propitious supernova appears.

* * * *

The pessimist believes (and that is the operative word) that a wave of depression can overwhelm, like a tsunami, an armada of potential fortitude. The optimist believes possibility can launch a fleet to discover new worlds.

* * * *

The locus or shortest distance between two differing points of view is a straight line, which, whilst keeping both poles apart, joins them. The length and density of the line keeping them apart, is determined by the potency of the respect and tolerance of a differing view, held by each party for the other. Once the connection is established, the firmer the line, the more stable and effective is the dialogue.

* * * *

'Let' allows for anything, so a human 'letter' always anticipates any eventuality.

* * * *

When you've screwed up, screw up and start again.

* * * *

In the Race of Life, if you're trying to be The Best, give up – you've already lost. In the Race of Life, if you're trying to be the best you can be, keep going – you're winning.

* * * *

Many will be surprised to discover that, far more of us have the capacity to think profoundly, than we might imagine.

PRAYER

So often, when people think of prayer, the image they have is of an elaborately robed priest in a church, possibly swinging a censer, and solemnly chanting an incantation in an ancient tongue. In reality, I usually see prayer as simply a conversation between two people, who enjoy an intimate relationship with each other — me and God!

Yes it is solemn — I am mindful that, in prayer, I am entering the holy presence of Almighty God, the majestic maker of heaven and earth and all things visible and invisible. You can't get any more solemn than that!

Yes it is simple — I know that, in prayer, I am where my Heavenly Father is waiting for us to talk together, chat if you like. Jesus referred to God the Father as 'Abba', the Aramaic for 'Daddy'. This indicates the close, intimate relationship, which God (as our father) wants with us — His children. It also shows us that God wants us to have the same childlike trust, which a young child has in his or her 'Daddy'. You can't get any more simple than that!

One day, after watching Jesus praying, one of the disciples said to him, "*Lord, teach us to pray.*" Clearly, the disciples had recognised the importance of prayer. The response Jesus gave to this request was: "*When you pray say.*" He then went on to give us the first wonderful rendition of what we know as 'The Lord's Prayer': "*Our Father in heaven, hallowed be your name, your kingdom come, may your will be done, on earth as it is in heaven. Give us each day our daily bread. Forgive us our sins, for we also forgive everyone who sins against us. And lead us not into temptation but deliver us from the evil one.*"

How many times have I recited that prayer, over the last sixty plus years? Certainly, it would have been at least nearly every day at school for ten years, and nearly every Sunday for more years than that. This means, I must have said it at least 2,000 times! But, it was only the other day, that I realised when I pray this prayer, how God-focussed and yet self-centred this 'model' prayer is. The first twenty three words are essentially

God-focussed. The next thirty three are, in the best meaning of the word: 'self-centred'.

Why is this? Could it be that Jesus wanted to emphasise that God's greatest desire is to have an intimate relationship with us as individuals? Is this the prime purpose of prayer, for you and I (as individuals) to enjoy communion with our Creator? I am more convinced this may be so, after reading the following definition of communion: *the sharing or exchanging of intimate thoughts and feelings, especially on a mental or spiritual level.*

When we look at some of the prayers recorded in the Bible, so many of them follow this pattern. For example, check out the following: Jabez — 1 Chronicles 4:10; Jonah — Jonah 2:2-9; Mary — Luke 1:46-49; Samson — Judges 16:28; David — Psalm 51 and 139.

Prayer then, is very much an individual affair and the way we pray will reflect our personality. Although not an exact science, I found using the Myers-Briggs Type Indicator helpful in understanding how personality has a bearing on attitudes, preferences and interests. If you would like to find out more about your personality type, visit: http://www.truity.com/test/type-finder-research-edition

I was especially interested, when I learned how being the sort of person I am, can have a bearing on my prayer life. Again if you're interested in this aspect, visit: http://www.schoolethos.ie/node/99

and https://www.freshexpressions.org.uk/guide/discipleship/starts/personality

I particularly liked the Fresh Expressions webpage, in that it included a note of caution: *The application of Myers-Briggs to spirituality and discipleship is more complex than this short summary might suggest. Yet despite its limits, might this summary suggest some possibilities?*

According to one prayer and personality website, my personality type suggests that I tend to be curious, insightful, imaginative and creative; I dare to dream, am committed to values, open to alternatives and constantly search for new and unusual ways of expression. Further, I may like spontaneous prayer from the heart, as well as enjoying contemplation on the beauty of God in the world. I may get many insights during prayer, and can have deep spiritual experiences of the presence of God. I will probably enjoy conversational prayer, and like to use symbols and poetic images. Lastly, I may use my creative imagination, to transpose the words of scripture to the everyday. I leave you, the reader, to decide how much evidence of this you might find in my writings.

Nothing I have said though, negates or diminishes the importance of intercessory prayer. The healthier the relationship, through prayer, between a man or woman, and God, the more that individual will be moved to intercede for others. Jesus said, *"Blessed are those who mourn* (mourn as God does the state of this fallen world, His creation), *for they will be comforted* (encouraged)."

You may find using these prayers yourself, to be helpful. Far more helpful though, will be to use them as ideas, templates for writing your own prayers.

Finally can I say, prayer is an adventure, a voyage of discovery. Just this morning, I got up early, to write a letter to God. The end result, which immediately follows, was totally unexpected. I've given it the title: 'Consider your cat?'

Consider your cat? — A Prayer Letter!

A Prayer: *A solemn request for help or expression of thanks, addressed to God* (Oxford Dictionaries).

A Letter: *A message which is written down or printed on paper* (Oxford Dictionaries).

For thus saith the high and lofty One that inhabiteth eternity, whose name is Holy; I dwell in the high and holy place, with him also that is of a contrite and humble spirit, to revive the spirit of the humble, and to revive the heart of the contrite ones. Isaiah 57:15 KJV

And why take ye thought for raiment? Consider the lilies of the field, how they grow; they toil not, neither do they spin. Matthew 6: 28 KJV

5.30am 19 February 2016

Dear Abba Father

Thank You for sending Your thoughts to me, earlier this morning. I find it incredible that, though You are 'the high and lofty one that inhabits eternity', You want to have a relationship with me. You don't know what this means to me but of course You do — for You know all things.

Lord, wait a minute! I am sitting in my lounge writing this and I have just heard our young cat, Misty (whom we have only had for two weeks) crying out. Someone found her in a plastic rubbish bag in a wheelie bin (a dumpster). She's in the conservatory, where we'd put her for the night. When I looked up, though it was still dark in the conservatory, I could see her white patch, and I knew she was there, sitting on the narrow window-sill. She had seen the light on, and had jumped up, so she could see me. Misty is desperate to be with me, but she can't be — unless I open the door.

Gosh Lord, what a great parable! I am reminded how often You must have called out to me, to be allowed into my thoughts, my life. Forgive me for all the times I've failed to hear You, for all the times I've heard You but ignored You. Thank You, for the many, many times, when I've heard You, and allowed You to speak into my life. That too is incredible. So too, is the fact that You wait for me to let You in.

When I think of how Misty was found in the plastic rubbish (trash) bag, in a wheelie bin, a dumpster, I am reminded of how you found me. Dead in my trespasses and sins, but You took me in. You cleaned me up, but more than that, You adopted me into Your family. You accepted me, welcomed me in just as in the same way, we have accepted, welcomed in and adopted Misty. Now you really care for me, feed me, provide for me and protect me — and, above all else, call me Your own. I hope she feels the same love and gratitude for me, as I feel for You — I really think she does, as much as cats can appreciate the enormity of that!

As I look back on my life, I realise how much of what has happened, is a result of what you have said to me. There are, I am sure, myriads of times, when I've acted in accordance with Your will and purpose, when I haven't appreciated it was because You had spoken into my life. I'm sorry too, that there have been many times when things have gone wrong in my life because I've not listened to You. But, there are many, many times, when I have been aware that You have spoken to me, and I have responded, perhaps with a word of comfort or encouragement for another, or doing someone an act of kindness. Maybe it's just like now, when I realised you had spoken to me through my cat. It is the realisation, You had spoken, which has caused me to say much more to You, than I had intended.

Thank You for reminding me too, that (just like my cat) You want to be with me, wherever I am. Thank You too for reminding me that (just like my cat) I am completely dependent on You, to meet my every need.

What Misty doesn't know, is that today I have to take her to the vets for an operation she needs. As she will have to have an anaesthetic, I won't be able to give her any food this morning. She will be expecting me to give her some. What will she think of me, when I don't give her what she's asking for? How many times has it been, just like that for me? You've known what I needed and, in Your love and wisdom, knowing what lay ahead for me, You have not given me what I asked for. Lord, forgive me for those many times, when I've not trusted You, because I think, You seem to have forgotten me.

In a little time, I will put Misty into the cat-box, to take her to the vets. She will wonder what's happening to her. She will be frightened. She may have to experience pain, certainly discomfort, but she will let me carry her into the unknown because she trusts me. I have always shown her kindness and provided for her, so she senses it will be alright. Father, help me to have such faith in You, as my cat has in me.

I don't know what lies ahead for me, but I know I can trust You. You have proven time and time again, that You are faithful, that You know what's best for me. Faithful God, Jehovah Jireh – The Lord who provides, thank

You for being here with me, as I step into the unknown that is today, that is my future — knowing that you will meet my every need.

Wow! How wonderful to know You are my Heavenly Father, and that we can speak to each other in the way we do.

Yours truly!

Peter

(Authors note! I picked Misty up later that day and the operation had gone well. Although at first she was uncertain of me, after I had given her the special post-operation pack of food from the veterinary surgeon, she seemed to sense that my intentions had been good, even though she may not have understood why things had happened to her in the way they had.)

Heavenly Father- God of grace and mercy

Heavenly Father,

I praise You because You are a God of grace and mercy. I praise You because You love me with an everlasting love. I praise You for Your patience and forbearance.

Thank You Lord for always being there, always being here. Thank You Lord for protecting me, providing for me, preserving me, but most of all, I thank You Lord for forgiving me, for accepting me, for loving me.

Lord I know I am unworthy of Your love. I confess, in so many ways, I sin and let You down. I know this grieves Your heart, please forgive me. I am sorry Lord for all I have done in thought, word and deed that has saddened You; for all I have failed to do, say or even think.

Forgive me for allowing my own sinful desires to crowd You out. I confess Lord, so often I choose to satisfy, to gratify the desires of the flesh, rather than to feed my soul.

Restore to me the joy of my salvation, and help me to hunger and thirst after righteousness. Help me to make You Lord of my life. May my first thought on waking be, to please You. May my last desire at night, be to know that I might have gladdened Your heart.

Lord increase my determination, to put things right in my life, to restore my priorities, to be free of the sins which so easily entangle me, and to live for You, not because I must, but because I want to.

I know you have forgiven me, and that in Christ I am accepted. Help me to live in the good of that, for His sake.

Bless me Lord!

Heavenly Father,

I praise You and worship You, for You are omnipotent, all powerful. There is nothing You cannot do in my life.

I praise You and worship You, for You are omniscient, all knowing. There is nothing You don't see, which is happening in my life.

I praise You and worship You, for You are omnipresent, everywhere. There is nowhere I can go but You are not there.

I praise You and worship You, for You are omni-sufficient, all creation belongs to You.
There is no need in my life, You cannot meet.

I praise You and worship You, for You are omni-benevolent, all good, all kind, all generous. There is nothing good, which I need, that in Your perfect time, You will not bless me with.

I believe that right now, there is an infinite store of blessing hovering over me, which You have prepared for me and which You want to pour into my life. I know that were You to release it all at once, I would be crushed. I know Your way has ever been to do things little by little, so that I will not be overwhelmed.

I believe that right now, You are eager for me to test You in this. So Lord, afresh, I gladly give you my life, all that I am, all that I have. In faith, I look to You to throw open the floodgates of heaven, and pour out so much blessing, there will not be room enough to store it.

Lord, I am so grateful, for all that You have done for me and all that You have provided for me. You are a faithful God, who has never failed me.

In a spirit of gratitude, I dare to ask today: Lord, will You bless me. Lord will You bless me, by keeping me. Lord will You bless me, by making Your face shine on me. Lord will You bless me, by being gracious to me. Lord will You bless me, by turning your face towards me. Lord will you bless me, by giving me peace.

Lord will You bless me. Lord will You bless me, by enlarging my territory. Lord will You bless me, by laying Your hand on me. Lord will You bless me, by being with me. Lord will You bless me, by keeping me from evil. Lord will You bless me, by keeping me from causing pain.

Lord will You bless me, by giving me more of Your Presence in my life. Lord will You bless me, by giving me more of Your Peace in my life. Lord will You bless me, by giving me more of Your Power in my life. Lord will You bless me, by giving me more of Your Provision in my life. Lord will You bless me, by giving me more of Your Protection in my life. Lord will You bless me, by allowing me to achieve more of Your Purposes in my life.

You have shown me Lord, what is good and what You require of me. That is to act justly, to love mercy and to walk humbly with my God. Lord, it is in Christ that I find out who I am and what I am living for. Long before I first heard of Christ and got my hopes up, You had Your eye on me, and had designs on me for glorious living, part of the overall purpose You are working out in everything and everyone.

Heavenly Father, today, may I throw open the door of my life to You, so at that same moment, I may discover that you have already thrown open Your door to me. May I find myself standing where I always hoped I might stand — out in the wide open spaces of Your grace and glory, standing tall and shouting your praise.

Dear Heavenly Father

I know it will be no surprise for you to receive this letter, but I just wanted you to know how I was feeling this morning. It's good to know I'm alive on the outside — but even better to realise I'm alive on the inside!

One day (today?), I know I will die on the outside and then I will discover what it fully means to never die on the inside. On that day (when it will be meaningless to call it a day!), I will be turned inside out. It will be dead interesting to discover the reality of infinity — eternally! Death has already lost its sting for me. Now there is no sting in my tale — for there is no tail, just endlessness — endlessly!

As I move out, and into my ever present future, I will pause and watch in wonder, as an orchid bud opens and, in the same instance, I will observe a galaxy coming into existence. I will witness how You, The Creator, forms every petal and every planet, with the same infinite, believable, yet unbelievable, care and attention to detail.

Perhaps then, I will step outside myself, and (for the first time) see my inside body. Then I will marvel at the same believable, yet unbelievable way, in which You have fashioned me. In no time at all, I will run a mile-less mile and climb the highest height-less mountain — and not be out of breath! Wow! The very thought of it, takes my breath away. I am really looking forward to seeing you soon!

With my love and grateful thanks, Yours eternally, Your son
Peter

Heavenly Father, Lord Jesus, Holy Spirit, the desires of my heart are:

To love You more,
To serve You better,
To hear You clearly,
To obey You always,
To please You constantly
To worship You and be with You forever!

Heavenly Father, Lord Jesus, Holy Spirit, help me to delight myself in You, for then You have promised, You will give me the desires of my heart.

Lord will You bless me, by giving me more of Your Presence in my life.

Lord will You bless me, by giving me more of Your Peace in my life.

Lord will You bless me, by giving me more of Your Power in my life.

Lord will You bless me, by giving me more of Your Provision in my life.

Lord will You bless me, by giving me more of Your Protection in my life.

Lord will You bless me, by allowing me to achieve more of Your Purposes in my life.

Personalised for Prayer

Sometimes, it is good just to take a passage of scripture, and 'personalise it', to use it as a prayer. This is what I have done with these extracts from Proverbs 3, 4 and 5. Read through these chapters, and decide whether what follows, is a prayer for you:

Father, help me to not forget Your teaching, but to keep Your commands in my heart, for they will prolong my life many years and bring me prosperity.

Let love and faithfulness never leave me; may I bind them around my neck and write them on the tablet of my heart. Then I will win favour and a good name in the sight of You and my fellow men.

May I trust in You with all my heart and lean not on my own understanding. In all my ways may I acknowledge You, so You will make my paths straight.

Help me not to be wise in my own eyes but to fear You and shun evil, as this will bring health to my body and nourishment to my bones.

May I honour You with my wealth and with the first-fruits of all my crops; for then my barns will be filled to overflowing and my vats will brim over with new wine.

As Your son, help me to not despise Your discipline or to resent Your rebuke, knowing You discipline those You love, as a father the son he delights in.

I will be blessed as a man, if I find wisdom and gain understanding, for Wisdom is more profitable than silver and yields better returns than gold. She is more precious than rubies and nothing I desire can compare with her. Long life is in her right hand and in her left hand are riches and honour.

Her ways are pleasant ways and all her paths are peace. She is a tree of life to those who embrace her and those who lay hold of her will be blessed. By wisdom You laid the earth's foundations, by understanding

You set the heavens in place; by Your knowledge the deeps were divided, and the clouds let drop the dew.

As Your son, may I preserve sound judgment and discernment, not letting them out of my sight; for they will be life for me, an ornament to grace my neck. Also, I will go on my way in safety and my foot will not stumble. When I lie down, I will not be afraid; when I lie down, my sleep will be sweet.

I need have no fear of sudden disaster or of the ruin that overtakes the wicked, for You will be my confidence and will keep my foot from being snared.

Help me to not withhold good from those who deserve it, when it is in my power to act. May I not say to my neighbour, "Come back later; I'll give it tomorrow" — when I have what they want with me.

May I not plot harm against my neighbour, who lives trustfully near or accuse anyone for no reason, especially when he has done me no harm. Help me to not envy a violent man or choose any of his ways, knowing You detest a perverse man but take the upright into Your confidence.

Although Your curse is on the house of the wicked, may I remember You bless the home of the righteous. Though You give the cold shoulder to proud sceptics, I know You give grace to the humble. I know too that the wise inherit honour, but You put fools to shame.

As Your son, may I always accept what You say, so the years of my life will be many. Continue Lord, to guide me in the way of wisdom and lead me along straight paths. In this way, when I walk, my steps will not be hampered; when I run, I will not stumble.

Help me hold on to instruction and not let it go; to guard it well, for it is my life. May I not set foot on the path of the wicked or walk in the way of evil men. Help me to avoid it, to not travel on it but to turn from it and go on my way.

May I remember the wicked cannot sleep till they do evil; they are robbed of slumber till they make someone fall. They also eat the bread of wickedness and drink the wine of violence.

May I always have before me the path of the righteous, which is like the first gleam of dawn, shining ever brighter till the full light of day. Whereas the way of the wicked is like deep darkness; they do not know what makes them stumble.

Father help me pay attention to what You say and to listen closely to Your words. May I not let them out of my sight but keep them within my heart; for they are life to those who find them and health to a man's whole body.

Above all else, help me guard my heart, for it is the wellspring of life. May I put away perversity from my mouth and keep corrupt talk far from my lips.

Let my eyes look straight ahead and my gaze be directly fixed on the level path You have shown me, only taking the way that is firm, not swerving to the right or the left but keeping my feet from evil.

Heavenly Father, as Your son, help me pay attention to Your wisdom, to listen well to Your words of insight, so that I may maintain discretion and my lips may preserve knowledge. May I never forget that my ways are fully in Your view and You examine all my paths.

'*Redeeming Love*', a wonderful love story, written by Francine Rivers, is based on the Book of Hosea. Francine takes the story and transposes it to a setting in the 1850s Gold Rush in California. I find using and adapting Scripture, as a basis for prayer, can be really helpful. I wrote the following prayer by simply using two verses from Hosea and verses from Isaiah 30:

Therefore I am now going to allure her; I will lead her into the wilderness and speak tenderly to her'. Hosea 2:14

I will plant her for myself in the land; I will show my love to the one I called 'Not my loved one.' I will say to those called 'Not my people,' "You are my people"; and they will say, "You are my God."' Hosea 2:23

In repentance and rest is your salvation, in quietness and trust is your strength. Isaiah 30:15

Yet the Lord longs to be gracious to you, he rises to show you compassion. For the Lord Is a God of justice, blessed are all who wait for him. People of Zion, who live in Jerusalem, you will weep no more. How gracious he will be when you cry for help! As soon as he hears, he will answer you. Although the Lord gives you the bread of adversity and the water of affliction, your teachers will be hidden no more; with your own eyes you will see them. Whether you turn to the right or to the left, your ears will hear a voice behind you, saying, "This is the way; walk in it." Isaiah 30:18-21

Heavenly Father,

You have declared that you will allure me and lead me into the wilderness, to speak tenderly to me. At such times, You will say to me, "You are my son". Then, I will respond to You, saying, "You are my God.'

Lord, You are very mindful of the many ways (and times), in which I have turned away from You. Yet you have never turned away from me. Your desire, whenever I have turned my back on you and wandered off, has been to win me back, as though I was a prize worth winning. Lord I find that incredible.

Thank you Lord for every time you have sought to allure me, to draw me back to Yourself. Thank you too, for every time you have led me into the wilderness to speak tenderly to me.

Thank you that even in the wilderness, I can discover that repentance and rest is the salvation You provide and in quietness and trust I can find the strength You give.

I know too, that your longing to be gracious to me is constant and you move swiftly to show me compassion. I know I will be blessed if I wait for You; please help me to be patient and have faith in Your perfect timing.

I am certain that whenever I cry to You for help, You will graciously hear me. At such times, I can be sure you will answer me.

Lord, I know there will be times in the wilderness, when the sustenance You provide will be the bread of adversity and the water of affliction. This seems strange and unattractive provision. However, I believe at such times, I will learn valuable lessons.

You remind me, that when I don't know which direction to take, I have only to ask You for guidance. When I come to a fork in the road, I can be sure the Holy Spirit will whisper in my ear, "This is the path to take."

Lord, help me to respond positively to Your leading, Your provision and Your direction, even when they seem unusual and strange. Thank you too, that life with You can be an exciting adventure into the unknown, where I will be surprised at Your amazing provision.

Prophecy

Can I just share a few more words about prophecy. I believe that God imparts insights (not necessarily concerning future events), to encourage and inspire His people. For me, this means thoughts, pictures or impressions, come into the mind, which have a quality of otherness to them. With them comes a prompting, almost a compulsion, to share these with others. I don't claim to have any special ability and certainly don't feel any more qualified than others to do so. Rather, I believe God has given everybody such a gift and I seek to encourage and inspire others to share things, which they believe God has put on their hearts.

Prophecy isn't just speaking words, I believe our actions, our lifestyles are all meant to be prophetic, the outworking of lives that have been touched by God. The Bible states that all prophecy should strengthen, encourage or comfort, i.e. it edifies. Traditionally, strengthening, encouragement, comforting and edification are seen, quite rightly, to have connotations of gentleness. However, there are times when prophecy may have a harsher edge or be more forcibly directional. Much Old Testament prophecy was like this. Thankfully, I have never felt God has given me words of this ilk but I don't rule it out. Nevertheless, if I felt He had, I know I would need to have His wisdom to know how, when and with whom to share it.

At the end of the day, it is for others to discern whether what I share is from God or not but I would hate anything I said to cause anyone undue distress, hurt or harm. For me, God is a gentle God. I understand, that often the meaning of the Greek word for 'gentleness', in Scripture, is 'power under control'. All in all, I would rather I made the mistake of straying on the gentle side than on the other.

* * * * *

The following are words I have shared in Christian meetings believing that God wanted to say something through them. Maybe as you read them through, God will speak to you through them too.

The Huge Gulf

There is a huge gulf between My great desires for you, and your meagre expectations.

I desire to give you bread, you expect to be given a stone.
I desire to give you a fish, you expect to be given a snake.
I desire to forgive you, you expect to be condemned.
I desire to receive you, you expect to be rejected.
I desire to extend you, you expect to be limited.
I desire to prosper you, you expect to be impoverished.
I desire to enjoy you, you expect to be unappreciated.
I desire you to be My child, you expect to be no more than a servant.
I desire that you should dwell in peace, you expect to live in fear.

Through my Son, Jesus Christ, I have bridged the gulf between my great desires, and your meagre expectations. As an act of your will, in worship, move over from the side of your meagre expectations to the side of My great desires for you.

In the right place

You must accept you cannot be in two places at once, so you are foolish to believe you can be or that you can pretend to be. You need to acknowledge to Me, to others and to yourself, where you are. That is not necessarily where you think you should be, nor even where you would choose to be. Often you have chosen to be where you are through rebellion, through sin, through stubbornness or through not hearing My voice, or sensing My direction.

At the same time, I want you to believe that I am omnipresent, therefore I can be in a myriad places at once. I am with you where you are, and, even though in one sense, as you rightly discern, you are not in the right place, nevertheless, because I am with you, I make it the right place for you to be — at this time.

As well as being with you where you are, I am searching for you. I am searching for you, not because I need to find you, for where can you go to flee from My presence? No, I am searching for you when I know where you are, because you need Me to find you. This is in order that you can find yourself and discover where you are. Only then, will you know why I have allowed you to end up where you are.

I am searching for you too, because you have hidden yourself from Me, by being where you are. It will be in My coming to you, and calling out to you, "Where are you?", as I called to Adam and Eve, that like them, you will discover the futility, the foolishness of being where you are. Then too, your true location will be revealed to Me, to others and to yourself.

In that sense, where you are, is not the right place for you to be but I am the One who works in "all things". For this is the right place for the things you think and feel to come out. Though many things you think and feel are not right, it is right that they come out and are expressed, so that you understand you cannot stay where you are but that you need to move, to where I want you to be.

Empty yourself, so I can fill you!

I invite you to empty yourself of this world, and allow Me to open the windows of heaven, and fill you to overflowing with My blessings. I want to encourage you to empty yourself of all that has filled your life, your mind, your emotions and your spirit, which was not of Me. Before you do so, recognise that though they were not of Me, I have used them for good, to draw you to Me.

So, empty yourself of your tiredness, your weakness, your distress, your sorrow, your sickness, your troubles, your concerns, your sadness, your anger, your frustrations, your loneliness, your restlessness, your reckless-ness, your bitterness, your fears, your darkness – indeed all that has pre-occupied and crippled you; yes, even your sin.

Allow Me now, to fill you with My energy, My power, My comfort, My joy, My healing, My peace, My wisdom, My gentleness, My contentment, My patience, My understanding, My light, My truth, My companionship, My teaching, My parenting, My protection and My provision – indeed all that you have need of and all that you desire in your inmost being, for you are Mine, bought at a price paid for by My Son. Most of all though, I want to fill you with My love, My mercy and My grace because it was for this purpose My Son poured out His life, and to this end, I have poured out The Holy Spirit.

Let your body, your mind, your emotions and your spirit rejoice as you do this – both as you empty yourself but more especially as I fill you to overflowing, so that others may be blessed and I will be glorified.

Don't be anxious!

(Another example of prophecy as simply a reworking of Scripture)

Don't be anxious about anything, not even what you will eat or what you will drink. Think about how the birds are fed, although they neither plant nor harvest.

Don't be anxious about anything, not even what clothes you will wear. Think how beautifully the flowers are clothed, although they neither weave nor sew.

If I, Your Heavenly Father, feed the birds and clothe the flowers, how much more will I look after you. Feed on the Bread of Life and drink of the Living Waters. Be clothed in the garments of righteousness and praise. Seek Me and My Kingdom, so My glory will shine through you.

(Another reworking of passages of Scripture,
I felt The Holy Spirit wove together)

My desires for you

I want to bless you and keep you. I want to make My face shine upon you and be gracious to you. I want to turn My face towards you and give you peace.

I want to bless you and extend your borders. I want My hand to be with you, to keep you from evil, so that you will not cause pain.

For I know the plans I have for you, plans to prosper you and not harm you, plans to give you hope and a future. You will seek Me and find Me, when you seek Me with all your heart. You will call and I will hear you, then I will be found by you and will listen to you.

Come to Me, all of you who are weary and burdened, and I will give you rest. Take My yoke upon you and learn from Me, for I am gentle and humble in heart, and you will find rest for your souls. For My yoke is easy and My burden is light.

Peace I leave with you; My peace I give you. I do not give as the world gives. Do not let your heart be troubled and do not be afraid.

Behold I make all things new

(Sometimes, God may give you a song, such as the one I believe He gave me here. I know it took a lot for me to start it, when I'd never done anything like it before. Indeed, when I believe He has given me a song, I still hesitate to start. What is remarkable though is how, as I begin to sing, I suddenly feel empowered to sing out, uninhibited and the words and music just flow.)

Behold, I will make all things new.
Behold, I will make all things new.
I will rebuild all that life has destroyed;
Behold, I will make all things new.

I will make everything beautiful in its time.
I will make everything beautiful in its time.
You may not see this now, but
I will make everything beautiful in its time.

Fear not for I am with you.
Fear not for I am with you.
I will hold you close in my arms,
So, fear not, for I am with you.

Trust in me, though the sun is not shining.
Trust in me, though the sun is not shining.
Soon the clouds will be removed, therefore
Trust in me, though the sun is not shining.

Let me have my gentle way

(Another song. I think the word 'let' is one of the strongest, yet gentlest, words God can speak into your life because it's a bidding, an instruction with the potential for actualisation. This is why this blessed me.)

Let me have my gentle way in your life.
Let me have my gentle way in your life.
Let me lay my gentle hand of love on you.
Let my gentle love rule in your life.

Let me have my gentle way in your life.
Let me have my gentle way in your life.
Let me lay my gentle hand of peace on you.
Let my gentle peace rule in your life.

Let me have my gentle way in your life.
Let me have my gentle way in your life.
Let me lay my gentle hand of mercy on you.
Let my gentle mercy rule in your life.

Let me have my gentle way in your life.
Let me have my gentle way in your life.
Let me lay my gentle hand of healing on you.
Let my gentle healing rule in your life.

Warts and all

You are what I intended you should be – warts and all. Your weaknesses, your failings, your blemishes, are as important aspects of your nature, as are your strengths, your successes and every positive aspect of your personality, character and nature.

Don't allow your weaknesses to be a hindrance but rather a spur, a help, an encouragement to what I can accomplish in your life.

Don't let your failures be a blockage to your progress but rather stepping stones in advancing my purposes in your life.

Don't see your blemishes as evidence of disqualification but rather see them as a reminder that I accept you, despite all that you were and all you have done.

I am a transforming and redeeming God. Behold the old things, which I declare dead, I have resurrected, and I have made them new. For my intention has ever been, to take that which the World intended for evil, and to use it for good – your good and My glory.

Take hold of My hand
(Another song)

Take hold of My hand and let me lead you.
Let me lead you through your troubles.
Let me lead you through your heartaches.
Let me lead you through your sorrows.
Take hold of My hand and let me lead you.

Take hold of My hand and let me lead you.
Let me lead you through the darkest valley.
Let me lead you through to truth.
Let me lead you through to forgiveness.
Take hold of My hand and let me lead you.

Take hold of My hand and let me lead you.
Let me lead you through to new pastures.
Let me lead you through to fullness of life.
Let me lead you through to life everlasting.
Take hold of My hand and let me lead you.

An Adventious God

Suddenly a great company of the heavenly host appeared with the angel, praising God and saying, "Glory to God in the highest heaven, and on earth peace to those on whom his favour rests."
Luke 2:13-14

When Jesus entered the temple courts, he began to drive out those who were selling. "It is written," he said to them, "My house will be a house of prayer; but you have made it a den of robbers."
Luke 19:45-46

I learned a new word this week: Adventious. It comes from the same root as advent, which means coming or arrival. But, adventious is an adjective, which has the added meaning of coming from outside, appearing in an unusual place or different way.

I felt God remind me, that He is an adventious God. He sometimes dramatically breaks into situations, like in those two readings from Luke. However, more often He comes in quietly, unobtrusively, gently, but always in a timely, and effective way.

Some times, He comes in unexpected ways or through unexpected people (like the boy Samuel, Naaman's wife's servant girl or the lad with the five loaves and two fishes).

He brings the heavenly into the earthly, the miraculous into the everyday, the supernatural into the natural, the extraordinary into the ordinary.

Usually too, he waits to be invited into our situations. He waits to be invited into our situations, as a group of His people. He wants to bring His harmony into our discord, His purposes into our confusion, His resolution into our differences, His flexibility into our rigidity, His ways through our impasses.

For us as individuals he wants to bring, His tranquillity into our turmoil, His reassurance into our fears, His joy into our sorrow, His healing into our sickness, His certainty into our confusion, His provision into our need, His correction into our errors, His forgiveness into our sin. His answers into our questions and so much more — the list is endless.

He wants to bring His solutions into our problems, into our lives, this week, but more importantly, He wants to do it now!

Are you ready to invite him in?

God's plans are greater than ours

(The following is a picture I felt God gave me, as our fellowship was starting a building project)

I was looking out on a huge building site, with a wide highway running through it. This highway stretched as far as I could see into the distance. When I looked behind me, I saw it also stretched back as far as I could see.

Then, a huge plan, a blue print was unfolded. Although I could see it was a plan, it was too huge to take in any detail but it seemed as if this highway was to be lined with buildings of all sizes. I felt God directed my attention to the plan of a particular a building, to the right of the highway. I sensed Him say, this was our part of His overall building plan, part of His wider purposes.

He seemed to stress the importance of this particular project, which He had entrusted to us, but at the same time was cautioning us to never lose sight of the fact that others too had their own projects, and were building alongside us. I knew it was not meant to be a construction competition but was intended to be more of a building cooperative. We should take pride in what we were building, but not boast about it. We needed to constantly bear in mind, we needed to stay within the boundaries He had set, so that everything fitted together, into His overall plan.

Whilst stressing how important our building project was and how big it was, in reality it was only a small part of His overall purpose of building a highway. He did not intend we should build a monument to ourselves, but rather we were to build a stepping stone for Him. The building was not to be an end in itself, rather it was to be part of the means to an end. The end was that His Glory should fill the earth and ultimately fill the heavens. So the project is big, but it is also small. It has a limited purpose in the span of time, but it is part of a plan of eternal dimensions and infinite proportions.

And, having done all, stand!

Another picture, I believe God gave me, and which really blessed me, and others that I have shared it with on occasions, was of a chessboard. My eye was drawn to a particular white pawn, one of the weakest pieces on the board. It was alone, well over on the opponent's side but it was protected from being taken by one of the other white pieces.

I realised that every time the opponent contemplated a move, they had to take the placement of that pawn into account. If you like, it held territory in the opponent's land. I felt God say that was how He sometimes used people, simply placing them to hold ground for Him, in the spiritual realms. I thought of a missionary, who may have been in a very lonely, isolated and perhaps hostile place. Maybe they felt they had not seen any fruit from their labours, the sacrificial giving of their lives. Perhaps it was someone who felt they had been left in a spiritual backwater in an inner city, and that their lives didn't count for much in the Kingdom of God.

I felt such people needed to know, God was using them strategically. Although they might not, as yet, see how God was using them, in the fullness of time they would. When they did find out, they would not complain that God had used them in that way. Rather they would rejoice, they had been counted worthy of the privilege of being trusted by God, to just stand firm and have faith in Him. They would know it had all been for a purpose — His purpose.

Sometimes, when we feel nothing is happening in our lives, we need to appreciate that God may be working out His purposes in the unseen, spiritual realm. Job had no idea he had been confounding and frustrating Satan, in the way he did. Through him, God was able to demonstrate, to the principalities and powers of darkness (including Satan himself), that when someone trusts Him, they will spiritually stand firm, even whilst suffering the fiercest onslaught of the enemy.

I feel privileged to have met many Christians, who considered themselves very ordinary people, who (completely unawares) were being used in extraordinary ways by God. Often, I've felt the Holy Spirit's prompting to share with them, that picture of the lonely, isolated pawn, who was doing God's will by simply standing firm.

Enlarge, Expand, Increase

The more you try to reduce Me to a size you can comprehend, appreciate, even manage or cope with, the more your expectations of what I can do in your life are diminished.

The consequence of trying to lessen the image, the understanding, the awareness you have of My greatness, the more you limit what I would be able to accomplish through you.

The reality is, I can only use the space, the capacity, the room you make for Me, in your mind, your heart and your spirit.

My desire is that My People will infinitely enlarge, beyond their comprehension, their appreciation of how great I am. For, I am The High and Lofty One who inhabits eternity.

As they begin to grasp My enormity, so their expectations of how I can use them, will begin to expand to immeasurable levels. So increasingly, they will realise the potential of what I can do, in and through them.

Do not settle for anything less than the impossible, the unachievable, the unimaginable, the unappreciable, the incomprehensible. If you do so, you settle for far less than Me.

For My thoughts are not your thoughts, neither are your ways my ways. As the heavens are higher than the earth, so are My ways higher than your ways and My thoughts than your thoughts.

Postscript

I gave this book the title: 'Practical Poetry, Prose, Prayer and Prophecy', because I wanted to encourage and/or provoke those who read it, to express themselves through the medium of the written word. Accordingly, here are some suggestions, as to how folk might do that. There are also a few further pointers, for writing in general, and for each of the categories.

The key, as in so many things, is in having a go, and to keep having a go. Don't be put off, if at first you don't succeed — keep at it. Don't be put off by negative criticism, but accept advice. Learn from others, read widely. Research how to write, learn all you can about grammar and punctuation. I have found text books on such matters written for children (they used to be called primers), helpful in this respect. If you're using a computer to write, it is good to use a spell-check and a grammar checker.

Make good use of a dictionary and a thesaurus. Online versions can be useful. A thesaurus is a book that lists words in groups of synonyms, similar words. What can you do, if you have used a word in a sentence or passage and you want to use a word that has the same or similar meaning? I usually do an online search by typing that word, followed by the word 'synonym'. For example if I wanted an alternative to the word 'love', I'd type 'love' followed by 'synonym', in the search box. If you come across a word you don't know the meaning of, look it up in a dictionary! In that way you build up your vocabulary and acquire a love of words. You may find sites such as wordsmith.org an enjoyable, daily way of expanding your word-store!

But remember, perhaps above all else, all writing is idiosyncratic. What is most important, is to just give yourself the opportunity to express yourself, through the medium of the written word. For the Christian, all that matters is that it expresses to God, how they feel about something, which is important for them, or simply something they want to say to their Heavenly Father.

By the way, writing style guides, such as The Chicago Manual of Style, would suggest that the above paragraph (perhaps like much of the prose in this book), is not well-written, from a grammatical and literary point of view. For example, such a manual would state that you don't start a sentence with a conjunction such as 'but', let alone start a paragraph. And, it's considered bad practice, to start a sentence with gerund. Looking up the meaning of 'gerund', as I had to do, when I first came across the word, will explain all! At this point, ever if they not already done so, a copy editor would be tearing their hair out.

Normally, if you were writing for wider publication, you would need to use the services of a copy editor. I would have chosen, as stated previously, to have had this book professionally, copy-edited, were it not for the fact that I wanted to stress that writing is a very individual thing. The more you write, the more your style, your grammar and punctuation will improve. Don't forget too, accepted styles are always being updated. For instance: The Chicago Manual of Style is in at least its 16th edition. Again, if you look at a wide cross section of well-known authors, you will find many examples of how they sometimes defy convention.

I find, especially the older I get, that there are times when I write a similar word to the one I meant or use the wrong tense. When I read what I have written back through, I often read what I meant to write, rather than what is there. I find it a great help therefore, to use a text-to-speech programme, which shows up such mistakes and also lets me gauge how well a particular passage flows. You may find the free version of *Natural Reader* useful in this respect.

Poetry

I cannot stress too much, how important it is to read widely. Nowhere is this more so than in regard to poetry. Read all the poetry you can, especially in this context, Christian poetry. Reading an anthology (particularly one which gives a good spread of both classical and modern poems), will show you the various forms poetry can take. You could use these as a template to write similar styled poems. About twenty years ago, The Lion Christian Poetry Collection' was published. I think it is now out of print but you may be able to pick up a 'used' copy on the internet, through someone like *Amazon*. Failing that, do an internet search on 'Christian

Poetry'. You may also find a rhyming dictionary handy. Try http://www.rhymezone.com — a freebie which does much more than just coming up with rhyming words!

Prose

Again, read widely. Just try writing about how you feel, especially when your emotions are heightened. Look at the world around you. Stand back and take in the scenery or look closely at something which catches your attention. Then simply commit your thoughts to paper.

I find scripture sparks off creative writing for me. You may have noticed how many passages of scripture I refered to or indeed used, in my first piece of prose. 'Sin, Shame, Sense, Salvation' drew on such chapters as: Genesis 3, Luke 19, Luke 15, 1 John 1, Hebrews 4, Colossians 3, Romans 8, Psalm 32, Isaiah 55, Psalm 16, Psalm 23 and John 14 at least.

Prayer

In writing prayers, you can again draw on Scripture. Some passages like Psalm 51 and 139 are already prayers, but you might want to paraphrase these for yourself. Even Psalm 23 lends itself to further personalisation. Alternatively, you can do what I did with a passage like Proverbs 3, 4 and 5 or personalise the prayers of Jabez, Jonah, Mary and Samson, which I mentioned before.

Don't forget though, Jesus, in the Lord's Prayer may have wanted to show us that God's greatest desire is to have an intimate relationship with us as individuals. If so, the primary purpose of prayer, for you and I (as individuals) may be to enjoy communion with our Creator. As I said, I am more convinced this may be so, after reading that communion can be defined as: *the sharing or exchanging of intimate thoughts and feelings, especially on a mental or spiritual level.*

If you think this may be the case, then just chatter away to your Heavenly Father, as any young child would talk with their Dad. I am sure God is not concerned about the grammatical structure of your prayers. He will just want to share in your joy and excitement, as well as hear about your concerns and worries. He welcomes your praise, appreciates your gratitude, and always wants to see what needs you are looking for Him to meet.

Prophecy

In 1 Corinthians 14:26, we read: *'When you come together, each one has a hymn, a lesson, a revelation, a tongue or an interpretation.'* If this is the case, as I believe it is, how can we know what we are to bring? I once had a picture come to mind, which I found helpful and shared in a meeting, concerning prophecy, and bringing contributions.

The picture was of an angler fly-fishing for trout. Imagine him (or her) standing, up to their thighs in water, in their waders. A long length of line, flicks out from the rod. On the end of the line is an artificial fly lure. The 'fly' lands on the surface of an area of water, where the angler anticipates trout are likely to be. This process is repeated again and again. Each time, the 'fly' rests on the surface for a short while, floating with the current, before the angler recasts. The hope is that a fish will eventually take the bait!

I believe we need to use a similar process, for discovering what God might want us to bring to a gathering of His people. During worship, just prayerfully 'cast' your thoughts out, and see what comes into your mind. It could be a passage of scripture, a song (even a child's chorus). Sometimes, it will be something you feel God wants to say to you and others, words of comfort or encouragement.

Maybe it will be a seemingly random word, phrase, impression or picture. You may not understand the significance of this — that isn't what's of importance. What is important is the sense, sometimes a firm feeling, that God wants you to just speak it out. At such times, for extra assurance, say in your heart to God: "Lord I believe you want me to share this. If that's so, help me to know when it's the right moment to do so." If that is your heart, in faith just open your mouth, and speak it out — when the moment seems right. God will honour that.

I realise such a process will be a great challenge to many church leaders, who have been trained to believe that they have sole responsibility for what is said (or sung), in the main church worship service. Too often leaders, especially those who are salaried, feel that they need to control services, as though the outcome, the way in which the service is perceived by others, is a reflection of how well they are performing as leaders. To them I would humbly say, stop thinking that it's all down to you. It is Christ's Church and the Holy Spirit is the One who will control our meetings — if we let Him.

Some church leaders will feel very threatened by this. If you have always had set liturgies, why not set aside a short period in a service, in which you invite members of the congregation to share what they think God has put on their hearts. Allow others to weigh it, and discern if it is of God. Encourage people to say to the person bringing it, that their contribution blessed them, if indeed it did. This will usually be at the end of the service, but sometimes a spontaneous, instant response, will bless not only the one who brought the contribution, but many others too.

Some time ago, we had a young man who had been coming to our meetings for many weeks. It was a setting in which we encouraged anyone who wanted to, to contribute. No one was sure where this particular young man stood faith-wise, though the gospel had often been shared at gatherings where he had been present. Suddenly, one morning he started praying. His prayer was very simple, almost childlike but the effect that it had on the rest of us was awesome. It left us in no doubt that he was born again, and we rejoiced at this confirmation of his faith in Jesus.

I remember too, where in a church service, a youngster of about eight or nine years of age, came out to the front, uninvited, and read a Psalm. The particular Psalm, and the way in which he read it, left everyone else acknowledging that it was a truly anointed moment, and indicated, that for that brief time, he was leading the church. Was it Holy Spirit inspired? Was it scriptural? Perhaps, as Isaiah 11:6 says, there will be times when: *a little child will lead them*!

Just one more example of how God delights to use unexpected people. *At that time, the disciples came to Jesus and asked, "Who, then, is the greatest in the kingdom of heaven?" He called a little child to him, and placed the child among them. In addition, he said, "Truly I tell you, unless you change and become like little children, you will never enter the kingdom of heaven. Therefore, whoever takes the lowly position of this child is the greatest in the kingdom of heaven. Moreover, whoever welcomes one such child in my name welcomes me.* Matthew 18:1-5. It is quite thought provoking, isn't it? If God can use a donkey (Numbers 22:28-31), how much more is He likely to use a little child or the most unheralded among us.

A few days after writing the piece above, about the fly-fisherman, the picture came to mind again (whilst I was taking a shower). I thought how I sense God is often like a fly-fisherman, in his dealings with me. In Isaiah 55:10-11, we read: '*As the rain and the snow come down from heaven, and do not return to it without watering the earth and making it bud and flourish, so that it yields seed for the sower and bread for the eater, so is my word that goes out from my mouth: it will not return to me empty, but will accomplish what I desire and achieve the purpose for which I sent it'.* When God knows I am in a receptive state, He casts out His word and waits for me to recognise it, and like the fish, take the bait. Not that He is teasing me or trying to catch me out, He simply wants me to learn how to listen out for Him and respond, when He speaks.

* * * * *

What more can I say? I think that is it, except to say I'd love to hear from you, if what I've written has prompted you to write. Please feel free to send anything you've written to me at trustandshare@btinternet.com and I will be delighted to publish it on my website — www.peterjfarley.org. Let me know if you want to include your email with details about yourself, which you would like to appear with your work. This will enable people to let you know when your words blessed them.

May the Holy Spirit Himself, anoint your words and richly bless you, as you seek to glorify Jesus.

Yours in Him
Peter

Lightning Source UK Ltd.
Milton Keynes UK
UKOW06f2158280616

277278UK00003B/13/P